4

TROLL NATION

HOW THE RIGHT BECAME TRUMP-WORSHIPPING MONSTERS SET ON RATF*CKING LIBERALS, AMERICA, AND TRUTH ITSELF

AMANDA MARCOTTE

FOREWORD BY DAVID TALBOT

Hot Books

Skyhorse Publishing books may be purchased in bulk at special discounts
for sales promotion, corporate gifts, fund-raising, or educational
purposes. Special editions can also be created to specifications. For details,
contact the Special Sales Department, Skyhorse Publishing, 307 West 36th
Street, 11th Floor, New York, NY 10018 or info@skyhorsepublishing.com.

Hot Books Press® and Skyhorse Publishing® are registered trademarks of
Skyhorse Publishing, Inc.®, a Delaware corporation.

Visit our website at www.skyhorsepublishing.com.

10 9 8 7 6 5 4 3 2 1

Library of Congress Cataloging-in-Publication Data has been applied for.

Cover design by Brian Peterson

Print ISBN: 978-1-5107-3745-7
Ebook ISBN: 978-1-5107-3746-4

Printed in the United States of America

Contents

Foreword

By David Talbot

The world is burning, and yet the firelight illuminates the way out. The times are dire, even catastrophic. Nonetheless we can sense a grand awakening, a growing realization all around the globe that "people have the power, to dream, to rule, to wrestle the world from fools" in the prophetic words of Patti Smith.

But in order to rouse ourselves from the nightmares that hold us in their grip, we need to know more about the forces that bedevil us, the structures of power that profit from humanity's exploitation and from that of the earth. That's the impetus behind Hot Books, a series that seeks to expose the dark operations of power and to light the way forward.

Skyhorse publisher Tony Lyons and I started Hot Books in 2015 because we believe that books can make a difference. Since then the Hot Books series has shined a light on the cruel reign of racism and police violence in Baltimore (D. Watkins's *The*

Beast Side); the poisoning of U.S. soldiers by their own environ-mentally reckless commanding officers (Joseph Hickman's *The Burn Pits*); the urgent need to hold U.S. officials accountable for their criminal actions during the war on terror (Rachel Gordon's *American Nuremberg*); the covert manipulation of the media by intelligence agencies (Nicholas Schou's *Spooked*); the rise of a rape culture on campus (Kirby Dick and Amy Ziering's *The Hunting Ground*); the insidious demonizing of Muslims in the media and Washington (Arsalan Iftikhar's *Scapegoats*); the crackdown on whistleblowers who know the government's dirty secrets (Mark Hertsgaard's *Bravehearts*); the disastrous policies of the liberal elite that led to the triumph of Trump (Chris Hedges's *Unspeak-able*); the American wastelands that gave rise to this dark reign (Alexander Zaitchik's *The Gilded Rage*); the energy titans and their political servants who are threatening human survival (Dick Russell's *Horsemen of the Apocalypse*); the utilization of authori-tarian tactics by Donald Trump that threaten to erode American democracy (Brian Klaas's *The Despot's Apprentice*); the capture, torture, and detention of the first "high-value target" captured by the CIA after 9/11 (Joseph Hickman and John Kiriakou's *The Convenient Terrorist*); and the deportation of American veterans (J Malcolm Garcia's *Without a Country*). And the series contin-ues, going where few publishers dare.

Hot Books are more condensed than standard-length books. They're packed with provocative information and points of view that mainstream publishers usually shy from. Hot Books are meant not just to stir readers' thinking, but to stir trouble.

Hot Books authors follow the blazing path of such legend-ary muckrakers and troublemakers as Upton Sinclair, Lincoln Steffens, Rachel Carson, Jane Jacobs, Jessica Mitford, I. F. Stone and Seymour Hersh. The magazines and newspapers that once provided a forum for this deep and dangerous journalism have shrunk in number and available resources. Hot Books aims to fill this crucial gap.

American journalism has become increasingly digitized and commodified. If the news isn't fake, it's usually shallow. But there's a growing hunger for information that is both credible and undiluted by corporate filters.

A publishing series with this intensity cannot keep burning in a vacuum. Hot Books needs a culture of equally passionate readers. Please spread the word about these titles—encourage your bookstores to carry them, post comments about them in online stores and forums, persuade your book clubs, schools, political groups, and community organizations to read them and invite the authors to speak.

We're engaged in a war of ideas, a war for the hearts and minds of the American people. For too long, this war has been dominated by Fox News, right wing talk radio and the bestsellers that they manufacture. And by the corporate-sponsored discourse of the liberal media—including the *New York Times* and NPR-blessed authors and pundits who keep their social commentary within acceptable boundaries.

It's time to go beyond this packaged news and propaganda. It's time for Hot Books . . . journalism without borders.

—David Talbot, 2018

Introduction

Troll

    1. to fish for by trolling

    2. a: to antagonize (others) online by deliberately posting inflammatory, irrelevant, or offensive comments or other disruptive content

        b: to act as a troll

                                      —*Merriam-Webster.com*, 2017.

The national tragedy that was the election of 2016, in which a conspiracy theory–minded half-literate racist demagogue named Donald Trump managed to defeat the eminently qualified Hillary Clinton in the presidential race, created its own mini media industry asking the question *why*? How had this human troll, with his mugging face, orange coloring, and pussy-grabbing ways, managed to beat someone who had a long career in public service and had clearly done her homework?

A number of theories were floated, including claims that white working class America was reacting to poor economic circumstances, even though the economy was far more stable than it had been when Barack Obama won in 2008 and job numbers were largely looking good. Some imagined it must have had something to do with Clinton herself, that she had somehow run a uniquely terrible campaign and was solely to blame for the loss. But the evidence for this is lean on the ground.

The sad truth is that Trump owes his victory to a very dark turn in American conservatism. Unlike right wing ideologues of old, who at least tried to portray themselves as stabilizing and constructive, the right in the era of Trump is a movement of annihilation. They are bigoted, sexist, and mean, and often don't even try to dress these destructive impulses up in the garb of tradition or religion.

They delight in cruelty for its own sake. Building something positive has no real value in this new right wing. Pissing off perceived enemies, such as feminists and liberals, is the only real political goal worth fighting for.

They are, in other words, a nation of trolls.

Trolling is a term that started on the internet, to describe people whose main purpose online was irritating other people. It's the sort of thing that people of all political stripes used to engage in, a casual bullying for its own sake that was low stakes. But as the boundaries between real life and internet life have broken down, and as the internet has become the primary form of political communication, trolling morphed into something of a right wing philosophy.

No longer do those on the right feel any need to offer a particularly positive vision of America. Even Trump's campaign slogan,

"Make America Great Again," was rarely backed up with an articulated vision of what, exactly, that greatness entailed. Instead, it was an angry yelp, aimed at liberal America. It's about tearing apart a new America that was becoming more feminist and racially diverse. When social progress cannot be argued against, its opponents instead turn to trolling. And Trump—ignorant, thoughtless, mean, barely literate—would be their leader.

Trump's election had the strangest of bellwethers: the world of video games.

It's hard to believe it now, but in 2014, a storm of controversy raged for months in the online world of video gamers and became the template for what has been deemed "Trumpism." Before there was Trump, there was "Gamergate," where the smaller but equally American community of video game players was torn apart as the same bitter white guys (and their sad suck-up female supporters) lost their minds because some women had opinions about video games.

To most people who witnessed it at the time, Gamergate seemed like one of those incomprehensible internet wars that fades as quickly as it erupts, but in retrospect, it was an alarming portend of the rise of Trump, the alt-right, and an America that now has torch-wielding white supremacists starting street fights in the name of fascism. It foretold a country where the American right has devolved into a nihilistic movement, prepared to tear down the country rather than share it fairly with women, LGBT people and people of color.

Like many historical calamities, Gamergate began because a young man did not accept it when a woman told him no.

In August 2014, a man named Eron Gjoni wrote a nearly 10,000 word essay about his ex-girlfriend, a video game developer named Zoë Quinn. The piece, which he posted online, was an incoherent train wreck of thwarted male entitlement, in which Gjoni obsessed about Quinn's sex life. Calling a girl a slut online is often enough to get the internet hoards to attack her, but Gjoni's real stroke of genius was in claiming Quinn's professional success was not a result of her talent, but due to her trading sexual favors for good press coverage.

The accusation, and this cannot be stated clearly enough, was flat-out false. (Quinn did date a journalist, but he never wrote about her work.) But it played off the resentment so many men feel when they see a woman who has more professional success than they do. The lie gave these men a comforting fiction to cling to, which is that women who excel aren't really talented or interesting, but instead must be cheating—using sex or liberal guilt or anything but their actual talents to get ahead.

It's the same myth that millions would later use to convince themselves that Trump was somehow more worthy of their vote than Clinton.

Gjoni shared his post on internet forums where a lot of young men had already gathered to complain about women who were gaining a foothold in the video game industry. The result was the stalker's dream: Hundreds, possibly thousands of young men (and some women!) became lieutenants in Gjoni's quest to punish Quinn for dumping him. They harassed and threatened Quinn until she was forced to leave her home.

The campaign continued to spiral even further out of control, as the online mob expanded the circle of harassment. The targets of the Gamergate are familiar to anyone who watched the rise of Trump. While women who were viewed as uppity were the main hate objects, accusations also flew against journalists, deemed corrupt and out of touch by the Gamergaters. People who advocated for gender and racial equality were sneeringly dismissed as "SJWs," short for "social justice warriors." The vitriol was always justified by a hazy nostalgia for the good old days, when video games were supposedly simple and didn't bother players with all this political correctness.

Gamergaters, one could say, wanted to make video gaming "great again."

While the entire debacle garnered a lot of media attention, mostly from journalists—including myself—who couldn't believe how *angry* so many young men were, one enterprising young writer named Milo Yiannopoulos saw an opportunity. He saw that Gamergaters were incoherent and unorganized, but with a little leadership, they could be whipped into a hard-right youth movement. Yiannopoulos got to work injecting himself into the middle of Gamergate, writing apologies for the movement on the far-right site Breitbart and riling up the harassment mobs on Twitter.

Mainstream conservatives tend to lean on arguments of tradition and morality in order to undermine women's progress. Older conservatives try to spin their sexist views in positive terms, claiming that putting restrictions on women's reproductive rights and job opportunities is about constructing a happy family life. Traditional conservatism is genteel and condescending to women.

Yiannopoulos, despite—or because—he's both gay and British, seemed to get why Gamergaters were different. He dispensed with the niceties of the past and embraced a politics of unvarnished resentment. He told angry young men that they were being terrorized by "an army of sociopathic feminist programmers and campaigners, abetted by achingly politically correct American tech bloggers," and gave his young followers permission to embrace the politics of destruction.

Milo didn't pretend to be motivated by sexual morality or family values. Instead, he wallowed in foul language and braggadocio about his sexual exploits. He told his readers that they were justified in their feeling that women had, by striving for equality, stolen something from them. He offered them an anti-feminism stripped of any pretense towards chivalry, instead giving them permission to embrace a politics composed of nothing but resentment and destructive urges. He let them believe that the minor bumps and bruises of young adulthood, such as career struggles or dating struggles, were the direct result of women's efforts towards equality—and that justified harassment and cruelty towards women in return.

Gamergate faded, but Yiannopoulos's star continued to rise. Mainstream media sources were fascinated by how he was selling a right wing politics that wasn't interested in the usual justifications of social order or religious faith. Milo portrayed himself as a rebel, framing destructiveness as subversion. He harnessed an army of young male supporters he cultivated by tapping their resentments towards women, and pointed their ire at targets, such as Muslim immigrants, that fit the larger Breitbart agenda of white nationalism.

It was Yiannopoulos who really grasped, for instance, that the 2016 reboot of *Ghostbusters*, which starred four women instead of four men, created a perfect opportunity to tap into a vein of male outrage. For every man who still can't believe women are allowed to reject him, for every male college student angry that a girl got better grades, for every sexist still bitter that a woman got promoted over him at work, Milo offered yowling about the supposed injustice of *Ghostbusters* as an opportunity for revenge.

Yiannopoulos called the movie "an overpriced self-esteem device for women betrayed by the lies of third-wave feminism." It was a perfect distillation of his immense powers of projection. It's his audience whose self-esteem is shattered by seeing women in the kind of comedic roles they wish to believe that only men are capable of mastering. And it's his audience that would rather tear the *Ghostbusters* franchise down by its ears than have to share it with women.

As with Gamergate, Yiannopoulos was a ringleader in the movement to destroy *Ghostbusters* through an online harassment campaign, a movement that unsurprisingly focused mostly on the one woman of color on the cast, Leslie Jones, who Yiannopoulos called "barely literate" and "another black dude."

Even Trump got involved, putting out a 6-minute video where he whined, "And now they're making *Ghostbusters* with only women. What's going on?!"

The harassment of Jones got Yiannopoulos kicked off Twitter, but his banning only seemed to reinforce the view of Yiannopoulos's fans that they are victims of a "politically correct" culture that supposedly wishes to suppress supposed truths about race and gender through shaming and censoriousness.

To be clear, neither Yiannopoulos nor the modern right writ large invented this idea of trolling the left as a political ideology onto itself. Plenty of right wing personalities laid the pathway for the idea that messing with liberals is a reasonable substitute for having a coherent political philosophy. Rush Limbaugh, for instance, has maintained a multi-decade career as a radio talk show host by focusing his show primarily on the subject of the alleged evils of liberals and why listeners should hate these ominous creatures.

But after decades of that kind of propaganda, trolling liberals is no longer considered just a fun sport, but the ultimate purpose of conservative politics. The idea of making a positive argument in favor of conservative values has atrophied, leaving only the desire to troll in its place.

Ultimately, Yiannopoulos's most lasting legacy will likely be in his support for the Trump campaign, which in turn helped a generation of resentful young men believe that voting Trump, who Yiannopoulos called "Daddy," was the ultimate way to troll the feminists and liberals they hate. That Trump had nothing positive to offer doesn't bother Milo and his fans. If anything, that is seen as a plus: Trump is the politics of destruction, personified.

"I can put up with almost anything from Donald Trump, because of the existential threat he poses to political correctness," Yiannopoulos told me when I interviewed him in October 2016.

"He'd rather grab a pussy than be one," Yiannopoulos said after a tape was released of Trump, apparently unaware of a hot mic, bragging about how he likes to kiss and grab women "by the pussy" without their consent. Sexual assault is of no concern to this new right. It angers feminists and puts women in their place, after all. What else do you need to know?

Milo and his millions of supporters embody the nihilism that defines the new right under Trump. They don't particularly care if Trump is a failure or incapable of doing or creating anything positive. He's just a human sledgehammer to wield against a world that is starting to question whether white men are inherently superior to the rest of us. He's revenge for every woman who wouldn't fuck them, every black guy that got better grades, every younger relative who wrinkled their nose at them when they had too many drinks at Thanksgiving and let loose with a racial slur.

"I could stand in the middle of 5th Avenue and shoot somebody and I wouldn't lose voters," Trump bragged while campaigning for the Iowa caucus.

It's a brag that rings true, at least for his most ardent supporters. Depending on whom he shot, they might even cheer.

But imagine if Trump got hit on the head and had a personality change that led him to declare that, in interest of rectifying hundreds of years of white supremacy, he was supporting reparations. Then, after all this time, his base would turn on him.

Both Gamergate and the Yiannopoulos-led campaign against *Ghostbusters* have much in common with the strategy Trump used to transition out of being a reality TV star and into politics: Birtherism, a widespread conspiracy theory on the right that holds that Barack Obama was an illegitimate president because he was supposedly not born in the United States.

Trump didn't invent birtherism, which writer Ta-Nehisi Coates calls "that modern recasting of the old American precept that black people are not fit to be citizens of the country they built." But Trump did use his fame as a tabloid fixture and the host of *The Apprentice* to repeatedly inject the conspiracy theory into mainstream media spaces that used to be hostile to the kind of people who breathlessly recite racist urban legends.

Starting in the spring of 2011, Trump appeared on Fox News, NBC, MSNBC, and CNN, claiming, falsely, that Obama was hiding his true birth certificate and that a "tape's going to be produced fairly soon" proving Obama was born in Kenya. Even after Obama, in an effort to shut down the Trump-fueled media chatter, produced the birth certificate, Trump kept at it, declaring on Twitter that the birth certificate is "a fraud" and suggesting Obama was having people murdered to cover up the truth.

Trump also started pushing the idea that Obama hadn't gotten into Columbia University and Harvard Law School honestly. Trump repeatedly claimed he would pay millions of dollars in a ransom to get copies of Obama's transcripts, clearly implying that Obama didn't have the grades and had cheated to get into these prestigious universities.

Trump's birtherism and Yiannopoulos's campaigns around Gamergate and *Ghostbusters*, are about saying, without coming right out and saying it, that women and people of color are inferior to white men. The implication of all these movements is that the success enjoyed by women or people of color is unearned and inauthentic, that people like them simply cannot actually be smart or talented or even legitimate enough to get that far. And that everyone else supposedly sees it, too, but are too cowed by the fear of being called "racist" or "sexist" to say so publicly.

This narrative has a special appeal to men like Trump, who aren't particularly special or intelligent. The idea that the unfit are getting elevated by "affirmative action" or "political correctness" allows such men to believe that they would be the stars and the much-heralded geniuses, if those undeserving inferiors weren't sucking all the oxygen out of the room.

Yiannopoulos himself was set to ride a narrative of white male victimization to the kind of fame and fortune that continues to elude his female or non-white peers in mediocrity. Even after he got kicked off Twitter, he secured a quarter million dollar advance on a book deal with Simon & Schuster and was starting to book high profile appearances on shows like "Real Time with Bill Maher," where he received a convivial welcome.

Then a video surfaced in early 2017 showing Milo decrying the "arbitrary and oppressive idea of consent" that legally and morally prevents adult men from having sex with 13-year-old boys, a social more he blamed on "the left." While celebrating Trump bragging about the sexual abuse of adult women was treated by many in both right wing and mainstream media as a joyous assault on political correctness, celebrating the sexual abuse of boys was a bridge too far. After all, most of the people in power had themselves once been a boy, vulnerable to sexual predation.

Yiannopoulos lost his book deal and most of his mainstream media support after that. Luckily for him, the landings for the oppressed wealthy white man tend, even in 2017, to be feathery soft. Yiannopoulos self-published his book and is getting a heavy promotion schedule at Breitbart. He also has a lucrative speaking career, getting paid the big bucks by conservative groups on college campuses who see booking him as a delightful way to troll the liberals.

Milo's career demonstrates that, in the 21st century, one doesn't need interesting ideas or any real talents to sell yourself as a thought leader on the right. All you need is an overweening sense of white male entitlement and a gleeful sadism in defending it. As long as you have both those things, nothing you can say or do, no matter how offensive or terrible, will cause an audience of bitter white men (and some women!) to pry themselves away from you.

Ask Milo's hero: Donald J. Trump. Or, as people now call him, "Mr. President."

Chapter 1

Political Correctness

Almost no other concept has been as great a gift to the American right as the myth of "political correctness," this widespread contention in right wing circles that a censorious left has somehow disallowed conservatives nationwide to enjoy their First Amendment–guaranteed right to be an asshole. This belief, that right wing mouths have all been sewn shut by a Stalinist left, played an enormous role in the election of Trump.

"I am so tired of this politically correct crap," Politico reported Trump saying to the biggest cheers of the night at a South Carolina rally during the campaign.

"They have put political correctness above common sense, above your safety, and above all else," he said in a speech in June 2016.

"I think the big problem this country has is being politically correct. I've been challenged by so many people and I don't, frankly, have time for total political correctness," Trump said during a Republican debate.

There are many other examples, but I'll end on that one, because it encapsulates the rhetorical sleight-of-hand so many on the right use to establish the myth of "political correctness." They conflate being *challenged* with being *censored*.

It's an argument that really should be self-refuting. If the conservative right to free speech depends on not being challenged, then, by logic, it requires ending the liberal right to free speech. After all, what are liberals doing when they challenge Trump, if not using their free speech to counter his?

Even setting aside the legal definition of free speech, the problem with the term "political correctness" is, in itself, a form of political correctness. What is political correctness, if not the use of shame and social repercussions to discourage certain forms of expression? But labeling someone "politically correct" is using shame and the threat social repercussions to discourage any expression the conservative deems overly progressive.

It's a very snake-eating-its-tail problem, but the illogic doesn't seem to register with the members of troll nation. As with most things in troll nation, the free speech posturing and claims to desire a rough-and-tumble public discourse are feints. The behavior of the right suggests that the real goal here is not free speech at all. If anything, it's an effort to escape engaging in real discourse, which always brings with it the threat of proving the intellectual emptiness of so many right wing ideas.

There's an evil genius to conservatives painting themselves as champions of free speech chafing against the censorious forces of political correctness. As long as people are arguing about free speech and whether or not it's being taken from the right, they aren't actually arguing about the ideas that conservatives are touting. The "political correctness" gambit allows right wingers to imply their ideas are just so scintillating that the scared lefties have to censor them, without ever having to prove the validity of those ideas. It's a damn good way to make bad ideas seem rebellious and compelling.

Nowhere has this become more obvious than in the growing community of overt white supremacists, angry "men's rights activists," would-be brownshirts and other assorted jackasses that Hillary Clinton memorably labeled the "deplorables" that have been empowered by Trump's campaign and election.

Spend five minutes reading some alt-right blogger expounding on the supposed threats to "Western civilization" or how men are the gender that's really oppressed or, god forbid, how the popularity of rap music is leading to "white genocide," and it quickly becomes apparent how, just on the basis of their arguments alone, they aren't going to make inroads with the public at large. And the alt-right knows this, which is why their public-facing events have been packaged not as showcases for their rancid political beliefs, but as "free speech" rallies.

Instead of trying to defend their actual arguments, the alt-right prefers to be seen defending their right to make those arguments. That very few people are actually trying to shut them down hardly seems to matter. If they can't get actual leftists with actual power, they will pull stunts to create the illusion of censorship where none exists.

This was how the violence in Charlottesville, Virginia—which ended in the murder of a woman named Heather Heyer when a white supremacist plowed his car into a crowd of progressive demonstraters—began.

A group of white supremacists and other fringe right figures descended on the city for a two-day protest, claiming, as they always do, that they are the victims of leftist oppression. In this case, the complaint was over efforts to tear down statues honoring Confederate leaders, including the one of Robert E. Lee in Charlottesville. Fringe right figures love Confederate statues, because, obviously, these statues are tributes to white supremacy. It's not just that the men depicted literally committed treason to defend slavery, though that certainly should be reason enough to tear the statues down. The statues were largely built expressly as a way to assert white supremacy.

As many historians repeatedly pointed out, most Confederate statues were built during times of heightened racial tensions— usually when black Americans were pushing for more rights or gaining economically, and getting lynched or terrorized in return. Most were built in the early 20th century, when the KKK was reforming and lynchings were on the rise, and there was another spate of statue-building in response to the civil rights movement of the '50s and '60s.

The Robert E. Lee statue in Charlottesville was built in 1924, at the edge of a prosperous black neighborhood, Vinegar Hill. It was less about memorializing anything special Lee had done, and more to send a threat to black residents who were seen as uppity for having economic success. Eventually, white Virginians made good on the implicit threat, and Vinegar Hill was razed and taken over.

It's quite clear that the reason that the alt-right feels protective of these statues is they continue to admire and honor the values these statues stand for, which are white supremacy and the terrorizing of black people. But those are hard values to defend publicly, so instead, the right tries to make the discussion one of censorship and free speech, by accusing progressives of trying to hide history.

This is a nonsense argument, of course. Europeans, for instance, do a fine job of remembering the history of WWII without littering the landscape with statues portraying Hitler as a noble Christian warrior. But as a rhetorical tactic, it works fairly well. As long as they're forcing an argument about speech and memory and censorship, the alt-right doesn't have to defend what it is about slavery and white supremacy they find so honorable anyway.

The one problem, however, was that the protesters that showed up in Charlottesville did a piss-poor job of keeping up the pretense that this was an anti-censorship rally. The torch-wielding mob chanted racist slogans, waved Nazi flags, and made it quite clear what these folks are really about.

But even after the mask slipped that far, Trump clearly thought he could get away with rolling out the script about how it's just a bunch of free speech activists sticking it to the politically correct.

"You had people in that group that were there to protest the taking down of, to them, a very, very important statue and the renaming of a park from Robert E. Lee to another name," Trump whined during a post-Charlottesville press conference. "You're changing history. You're changing culture."

Trump and the alt-right organizers' attempt to establish a narrative where oppressed white supremacists are enduring censorship at the hands of leftists failed him that time, due to the murder and the general inability of the alt-right crowds to keep a lid on their enthusiasm for fascism that day. But the strategy of framing their issue in terms of "free speech" and opposition to "political correctness"—instead of as simply naked enthusiasm for racism and misogyny—has made more headway elsewhere.

The strategy, in Charlottesville and elsewhere, has been simple: Hold alt-right rallies in liberal-leaning cities with large college populations, pretending that the rallies are in the name of "free speech," but which are in fact an attempt to recruit more people to a toxic ideology built around bigotry and fascist sympathies. Act in incredibly provocative ways, including starting fights, and then pose as victims of violent leftist thugs who use their fists in the name of censorship. Ideally, they also get universities or the city police departments to shut it all down, so they can then claim they are victims of liberal censorship.

It's a disturbingly effective strategy because, to be blunt, there are a small minority on the left who are willing to play their assigned roles in this little bit of fascist drama, as the censors and the violent thugs. Antifas, the name for a loose coalition of anti-fascist activists who believe in direct action like outing fascists and confronting them on the street, have been known to get into fistfights with the "deplorables." This is especially true in college towns, where there are a lot more young, idealistic people ready to do this sort of thing. And there are a number of people on the left who demand that universities shut down right wing speakers.

I fully confess that I belonged, to a degree, to that latter group. Not all right wing speakers on campus could legally be shut down, or should be, but it did seem reasonable to me to point out that "free speech" doesn't guarantee one a stipend or a speaking engagement at a prestigious university. Most of us don't get those things, and no one is taking our free speech, after all.

But I've come around to the view that the right benefits far more than the left when some right wing speaker is denied a speaking opportunity, even in the case where these speakers are touting racist or misogynist views. It's arguable that the only real reason conservative student groups bring speakers like Charles Murray, Ann Coulter, or Ben Shapiro to campus is to troll the left. Even conservatives aren't really that interested in these people's views. Their value exists only as objects of left wing ire.

Not to say that people shouldn't counter-protest or speak out. These folks have dreadful views, which should occasion resistance, and ideally mockery. By all means, people should turn out and raise awareness about their terrible views, and argue and debate those that have such terrible views. What they shouldn't do, however, is try to censor, much less resist, with violence.

In other words, the left should deny the alt-right what they want, which is to play the victim of the censorious left. Instead, the left should give them what they don't want, which is an actual discussion and debate about alt-right views, a debate the right knows they cannot win.

The propaganda value of playing the victim of the censorious left was most cleanly illustrated by the saga of (who else?) Milo Yiannopoulos and the University of California at Berkeley, a school whose reputation for left wing politics has made it an object of fascination and hatred for the American right—especially now that trolling and nihilism have become the dominant features of the right under Trump.

Milo's built most of his fan base by appealing to very young men—think high school and college age—who frequently mistake the bumps and bruises of adolescence for persecution. It's not hard to understand why pimply-faced awkward teenagers would rather hear that feminism is to blame for their dating woes than their own inexperience. It's easy to see how normal adolescent insecurity, when confronted by young, empowered women who are speaking their minds and hustling for good grades and good jobs, could feel alienating. They don't know that those young women also have fears, failures, and face dating rejection. All they see is "girl power" and they get mad.

Milo's bullying persona makes his young male fans seem powerful, and his sexual orientation makes them feel hip—they're not like those homophobic, sex-hating conservatives of old. They're practically liberals, right? They just think feminists and progressives have taken it too far and need punishment.

All of which means that Yiannopoulos has created for himself a robust college circuit speaking career. The appeal of bringing Milo to your campus lies not in anything he has to say, which is mostly a bunch of reactionary vitriol that Rush Limbaugh perfected decades earlier, but in the way he really angers those campus liberals. He draws out protesters and angry comments online and allows his fans to believe that they have somehow gotten the upper hand on those earnest young liberals and feminists.

It's a phenomenon that would cause sympathetic embarrassment for these young fools, if they weren't being so awful. These young alt-righters have universally confused getting a rise with taking the piss out of someone, and don't seem to understand how badly they've missed the mark.

Due to the alt-right strategy of going to liberal college towns in hopes of maximum provocation, Yiannopoulos had scheduled his Inauguration Day talk at the University of Washington in Seattle. Tensions were high, due to the national trauma—or sadistic glee, if you're alt-right—of watching Trump sworn in as president. The scene outside of Kane Hall got violent as pro-Trump forces and leftists clashed. In the melee, a woman named Elizabeth Hokoana, aided by her pepper spray–wielding husband, Marc Hokoana, shot a socialist protester named Joshua Dukes.

The Hokoanas claimed self-defense, but one witness—David Neiwert, a reporter for the Southern Poverty Law Center, who was at the protest as a journalist—told me that Dukes had been trying to use his large frame to break up fights, not engage them. The Seattle prosecutors agree, citing social media posts made by Marc Hokoana about how he couldn't wait to "start cracking skulls."

The College Republicans hosted the event. "The point, club members say, was to promote free speech," the *Seattle Times* reported.

Once again, "free speech" and "political correctness" create excellent distractions to avoid talking about the actual content of the speech in question. Reports indicate that the speech inside was rambling, but was heavily focused on calling progressive protesters "fat dykes" and arguing "girls are retards."

After that near-killing, the University of California at Berkeley decided to cancel Yiannopoulos's scheduled appearance in February. The school could not have given Yiannopoulos, who had generally been treated like an unfortunate fart by more mainstream right wing publications and venues, a bigger gift. Fox News gave him glowing coverage. The Conservative Political Action Conference booked him next to their usual crew of gay-bashers and abortion obsessives. Bill Maher brought him onto his HBO show. Even mainstream liberal publications ran chin-scratching articles about the value of free speech, largely ignoring the context that suggested they were being taken in by right wing propaganda.

All that immediately came crashing down, as recounted in this book's introduction, when a video surfaced of him speaking favorably of grown men having sex with young teenage boys. Conservatives were ready to declare themselves fans of the rough-and-tumble, anything-goes world of political rhetoric when minorities and women were the targets—but nasty words towards *boys* was another story altogether.

Still, Yiannopoulos believed, for good reason, that a white man is never down for long in American society. He managed to get millions of dollars from secret investors (reportedly the billionaire Mercer family, according to Buzzfeed) and got back to his job of trolling college campuses. Berkeley, where the bona fide free speech movement began in the '60s, was the golden goose.

Milo announced in August of 2016 that, the very next month, there would be a four-day, conservative celebrity-studded extravaganza at Berkeley called "Free Speech Week." Mysteriously, it was being hosted by a tiny—with no more than 5 or 10 members—student group called the Berkeley Patriot that had no existence before July of that year and only started its web pages after the announcement of this suspiciously large event.

As I documented for an investigation at Salon, there was a significant amount of evidence that Yiannopoulos and his student group never intended to have this event. The students kept missing deadlines for registering event space, and when prodded by the school, they kept coming up with obtuse objections to signing the paperwork. There also seemed to be no interest in actually booking speakers. A dazzling (by right wing standards) list of speakers did get released, but many of them, including Charles Murray, told reporters they weren't coming and others said they had never even been invited. A few who had tentatively signed on dropped out when they saw the chaos.

Perhaps Yiannopoulos thought that Berkeley would cancel his event again, giving him another opportunity to run to the media with a "help, I'm being censored by political correctness!" narrative. But the school had clearly learned its lesson from the February debacle. The university spokesman got out in the media heavily, emphasizing how much Berkeley valued free speech and how they bent over backwards to accommodate this event, despite all the delays and objections to finalizing the details the student group put up.

However, the school was unable to let students have some indoor space they requested, since the application had still not been finished a mere 9 days before the supposed start of Free Speech Week. This was enough for Milo, who immediately went hard on a social media campaign to argue that he was being censored, even though the school had permitted a large outdoor rally to proceed. By then, however, some reporters—including myself—had gotten the word out that the problems with Free Speech Week were from the organizer side, not the school's.

Unfortunately for Milo, the media blitz worked. Despite the yammering from Yiannopoulos and his supporters about "censorship," it was clear that no one was actually trying to suppress Yiannopoulos's half-wit trolling efforts. Without the sizzle of the censorship narrative, the size of the crowd that turned out was paltry and not particularly fired up. Yiannopoulos made a few tired remarks, took a few pictures, got bored and left. Free Speech Week, in the end, lasted less than half an hour.

The entire debacle is a perfect example of how central the narrative of "political correctness" is for the alt-right. Without it, they have almost nothing to buoy them up. The victim pose is the only way they can even try to conceal that their actual views are that of the bully trying to bring the boot down on the neck of minorities and women.

The willingness of this new, more nihilistic right to simply make up reasons to claim censorship was amply demonstrated in June 2017, when a heavily armed group of right wingers descended on Hermann Park in Houston, Texas. The protesters, under the name "This Is Texas," claimed they were there to defend the iconic statue of Sam Houston that adorns a gate in the park from the "Black Panther Party, Antifa & more."

Unsurprisingly, the whole thing was a hoax. The *Houston Chronicle* traced it back to a fake webpage purporting to be a Texas antifa group, but actually created by an alt-right activist. (The willingness of right wingers to hoax their own people is a common theme to many of these stories.) The statue itself has no relationship to Confederate nostalgia—while Houston was a slave owner, he opposed secession and the war.

And yet, even when they were told it was a hoax, the right wing protesters refused to accept it. The event went on anyway, and protesters swore up and down that they saw antifa lurking in bathrooms around the event, a face-saving delusion that is too pitiful to be enraging.

The grim truth is that these right wingers needed, desperately, to believe that they were somehow being oppressed. Openly having a rally to celebrate slave owners because they were slave owners is still, even in Trump's America, a line that is considered too gross to cross. So instead they came up with an elaborate pretext: Antifas want to tear down this statue because of slave-holding and we are defending it because "heritage" and definitely not because we really spend a lot of time thinking about how awesome it was that white men used to own slaves! No sir, definitely not that!

The story about how the right is being daily oppressed by political correctness fails on its own measure, to be sure, but the situation is made even more ridiculous by the sheer hypocrisy on display. As the next chapter will show, the grim reality is that there is a strong and powerful movement of politicized suppression of free expression—and by and large, it's coming from the right, not the left.

Chapter 2

Whose Political Correctness?

As I discussed last chapter, the conservative movement, in the Trump era, gets a disturbing amount of political cachet by framing themselves as champions of free speech and rowdy, no-holds-barred discourse, in contrast to the supposedly buttoned-up "politically correct" left. Even many liberal commentators take the bait, so eager to show how fair-minded they are that they fail to double-check if the stories of leftist censorship they hear so much about are true.

The reality is that the right's discourse around "political correctness" has served to create a wild double standard, where pundits are quick to accuse liberals of censorship while ignoring far more egregious attacks on speech by the right.

For instance, Jonathan Chait wrote what he clearly meant to be an expose of P.C. censorship on the left for *New York* magazine in 2015. But readers who expected a series of horror stories about Stalinist college administrators refusing to let students listen to Rush Limbaugh found instead that Chait's argument was a little less interesting. To wit, his thesis was that for conservatives to enjoy free speech, those on the left must silence their own tongues.

"A year ago, for instance, a photographer compiled images of Fordham students displaying signs recounting 'an instance of racial microaggression they have faced,'" Chait wrote in an outraged tone.

Chait used his essay to denounce professors who use trigger warnings, a hip new term for letting students know if study material has upsetting or violent images in it. He lashed out at students who protested microaggressions, a social justice for those small bigoted things people often say in passing. He whined about the term "mansplaining," a term used by women to tease men who like to hold forth at length about subjects they know little about. (The reader is free to draw her own conclusions about why Chait might be extremely sensitive to being told it's not cool to be a know-nothing bore.)

While Chait found a couple of extremely minor examples of censorship, by and large his essay was a long, whining diatribe about how those on the left should refrain from speaking out, much less protesting, to avoid bruising the easily hurt feelings of white men. In the very same essay, however, he vigorously defended a conservative student who wrote an offensive article in his school paper on the grounds of "satire."

What became quite clear is that there's a strong double standard, so ingrained that even some liberals don't see it: When conservatives say things that hurt the feelings of liberals, that's just free and rowdy discourse of the sort that our Founding Fathers enshrined in the constitution. When liberals hurt the feelings of conservatives, however, by calling out racism or sexism? Well, that's horrific "political correctness" and needs to be silenced post-haste.

The sheer, unadulterated gall with which this double standard is put forward was neatly illustrated in the space of a few short weeks over the late summer of 2017, after the events in Charlottesville reminded the public that the fake debate over "free speech" is often a fig leaf for a very real demand on the right to forward white supremacist ideas without public pushback.

In August, a Google engineer named James Damore briefly became a cause célèbre on the right when he emailed a 10-page screed across this company that got leaked to the press. While laden with ass-covering claims to belief in equality, the memo was an incoherent rant about how women are, due to biology, incapable of handling full equality with men. Damore was angry that Google had put forward efforts to improve gender and racial diversity, because women, in his opinion, are better suited to "jobs in social or artistic areas."

(Damore did not explain how, if women excel at artistic and social pursuits, men dominate industries like Hollywood and the music business, or why works by female artists only constitute 3–5 percent of the major permanent collections by American museums.)

Damore's piece was poorly argued, sourced to unreliable and cherry-picked references, and swiftly debunked by actual experts in biology and neuroscience. Honestly, that it needed debunking at all is a testament to how much more weight our society gives to bigoted arguments than arguments against bigotry. Any fool should have been able to see that a term like "mansplaining" had to be invented to describe exactly this genre of talking out of your ass that Damore's memo embodied.

Google ended up firing Damore, not because the company is some bastion of political correctness, but because most workplaces frown on it when employees mass-email their colleagues with rants about how a good chunk of them are physically incapable of competence. People need to get along with their colleagues, which is hard to do when you know for a fact that your coworker is sitting there glowering with rage because he thinks your job belongs to a man by biological right. Perhaps Google could have dealt with the problem by firing all the women instead, a solution that would have no doubt pleased Damore, but would have gotten the company in serious trouble with the EEOC.

So he had to go, a choice that would be common sense if Damore had insulted the intelligence of his coworkers because they are being cat owners, stamp collectors, or country western fans. But instead, he wisely targeted the intelligence of women, and so he found he had a supportive base with conservatives—a group that otherwise tends to defend the right of employers to fire their workers for whatever reason they like.

The *National Review* literally published two dozen articles on Damore, including David French declaring "identity politics" to be "incoherent and vicious" because of the firing. Scolding your coworkers for their failure to appreciate the inherent inferiority of women, as Damore did, does not rate as incoherent or vicious.

David Brooks of the *New York Times*, never one to be fond of workers' rights before, piously demanded that the Google CEO resign, arguing that "gender equality" is incompatible with "scientific research."

In reality, as science writer Angela Saini wrote in the *Guardian*, "There isn't a neuroscientist alive who can say with confidence which sex any given brain belongs to."

Suzanne Sadedin, an evolutionary biologist called Damore's arguments "despicable trash," a thorough debunking at Quora.

As usual with these kinds of debates, however, the low quality of Damore's actual arguments got somewhat concealed by the favored gambit from those on the right who know their arguments can't stand on their own terms: claims of censorship.

This had a stickiness in public discourse, due to Damore being fired for what he wrote. Liberals do generally get a little queasy at the idea of people's speech being controlled by employers exploiting their need for employment and have moved in some areas for legal and union protections for worker speech for just this reason. But there's no reason to take the bait in this particular case.

Even the most ardent supporters of free speech rights for workers draw the line when the speech in question runs contrary to the ability of the worker to perform the job duties they were hired to do. Making yourself unpleasant to work with by baselessly accusing your coworkers of incompetence qualifies. Damore didn't speak about his political views on his own time on Reddit. He didn't mention them in passing. He didn't speak broadly of his political opinions. He sent an email around that publicly undermined his female colleagues at their own workplace; that could be considered harassment or, at best, a direct attack on employee morale.

Either way, it took very little time for conservatives to show their deep hypocrisy on this issue. A month after Damore was fired by Google, a black female sportscaster for ESPN, Jemele Hill, tweeted, "Donald Trump is a white supremacist who has largely surrounded himself w/ other white supremacists."

Unlike Damore's screed, Hill's statement was blessedly short and blessedly based in truth. Trump, as the raving head of troll nation, is inarguably racist and won office by demonizing black people, immigrants, Latinos, and Muslims. Just a few weeks prior to this, he called the people who marched with Nazi flags in support of a Confederate statue "fine people." Like the writer Ta-Nehisi Coates impishly said on MSNBC:

> I think if you own a business that attempts to keep black people from renting from you; if you are reported to say that you don't want black people counting your money; if you say—and not even reported, just come out and say—that someone can't judge your case because they are Mexican; if your response to the first black president is that they weren't born in this country, despite all proof; if you say they weren't smart enough to go to Harvard Law School, and demand to see their grades; if that's the essence of your entire political identity you might be a white supremacist, it's just possible.

But debates about accuracy aside, Hill's tweet was different than Damore's memo, primarily because she wasn't talking about her own coworkers and their ability to do their job. Still, ESPN had a right to fire her and it's clear from some actions they took that they considered it—except that Hill's own coworkers stood up for her, which really undermines any comparison to Damore's attack on workplace morale.

Needless to say, all the right wingers who suddenly found cause to support the worker's right to political speech went suddenly silent when it came time to defend Hill for expressing her political opinion that was directed not at colleagues but at the actual president.

Things get really sticky, however, because Trump himself stepped into the fray. His press secretary, Sarah Huckabee Sanders, called Hill's comment a "fireable offense." Then Trump himself tweeted, "ESPN is paying a really big price for its politics" and demanded an apology.

While the right of employers to fire you for speech is a hazy area, there's a much more clear-cut attack on free speech going on when the president of the United States makes threatening demands that private citizens lose their job for criticizing him. Functionally, he's trying to use his government powers to deputize private employers into undermining speech that the constitution forbids him from directly punishing people for.

"When you have a government official saying to a private entity, 'You ought to fire somebody because of their political speech,' that raises very significant First Amendment concerns," Samuel Bagenstos, a constitutional law professor at the University of Michigan, explained when I interviewed him for Salon.

The whole incident, as well, shone a light on who exactly are the delicate snowflakes who can't handle blunt political discourse: conservatives.

"The problem for Hill isn't that the conclusion lacks a factual basis," Jamelle Bouie of *Slate* wrote. "The problem is that it offends certain groups of white Americans. It is, in a phrase, *politically incorrect.*"

Bouie went on to point out that the whining and crying of conservatives is a "force that shuts down frank discussions of racism and racist acts," and does so with far more effectiveness than a few college kids booing a right wing speaker ever could.

This was demonstrated amply long before Trump used the awesome powers of his office in an effort to punish a black woman for criticizing him. The over-the-top response from law enforcement to the Black Lives Matter protests that started in Ferguson, Missouri, after the shooting of an unarmed teenager named Michael Brown are a chilling example of how the right's claim to love "free speech" doesn't ever seem to extend to people making truly subversive challenges to the status quo.

In city after city, the police have overreacted to Black Lives Matter protesters, often gassing crowds or meeting unarmed protesters with a militarized police force. While there's no doubt that some protesters do things like break windows or throw bottles, the reality is that the police response has been repeatedly excessive and needlessly provocative. The police don't like what Black Lives Matter protesters are saying, and so often opportunistically seek any excuse they can to use government power to shut it down.

In one September protest of a police killing of a man named Anthony Lamar Smith, the St. Louis cops didn't even try to conceal their motivations, reportedly chanting, "Whose streets? Our streets!"

This desire to stomp out left-leaning protest has grown so out of control on the right that the idea of running over protesters with your car has become a meme in right wing circles. Cartoons and videos showing cars plowing into crowds of protesters became popular in the early parts of 2017. Even Fox News got into the game, publishing a video celebrating the idea of cars running over protesters in January 2017. Republicans in 6 states introduced bills to legalize running over protesters.

That all receded after Charlottesville, when a white supremacist went ahead and acted on the calls to run over protesters in an act that killed one woman and injured many others. But it certainly cuts against the idea that it's *liberals* who are the ones mainly advocating for violence to suppress free speech.

Trump and his supporters swivel from wanking about "free speech" and "political correctness" to demanding the silence of black people who disagree with them with dizzying speed. Trump, who was falsely claiming in February that "Berkeley does not allow free speech" ended up spending most of September castigating black celebrities for criticizing and trying to intimidate their employers into firing them.

Hill was just the beginning. During a rally in Alabama later that month, Trump denounced the NFL for not firing players who kneel during the national anthem in a silent protest against police violence, saying, "Get that son of a bitch off the field right now, he's fired. He's fired!"

(That Trump was pandering to racists was made all the more obvious by the fact that the person who started the protests, Colin Kaepernick, was, in fact, functionally fired. After he became a free agent, no team would hire him, and it's clear it's because he's politically outspoken. But he gets no David Brooks columns defending him, even though his speech doesn't hurt his team's ability to do their job. On the contrary, Brooks snottily denounced Kaepernick's protest by whining that "common rituals are insulted.")

"That's a total disrespect for everything we stand for," said Trump, who is known for his big mouth and utter lack of respect for anyone who isn't a rich white man.

Trump's outrage that black people talk back to him became an all-consuming obsession that ended up distracting him and his administration for days from dealing with the fact that Puerto Rico was devastated by a hurricane. As the island lost all its electricity and people died, Trump let loose with 14 tweets castigating NBA player Steph Curry and NFL players who criticized him or kneeled during the national anthem in protest.

These tweets went beyond disagreement with these players and shaded into attacks on free speech, such as when Trump said players "should not be allowed to disrespect . . . our Great American Flag" or demanded that NFL head Roger Goodell force the players to stand.

Players "MUST honor and respect" the flag said the man who swore an oath to protect the First Amendment rights of all Americans to make that choice for themselves.

What the legal recompense could possibly be when the president uses his power to intimidate private organizations into punishing speech that is legally out of his reach is still unknowable. This is relatively uncharted territory in American politics, due to the pretty strong legal protections offered by the First Amendment. Plus, Trump's bellowing efforts to strong-arm ESPN and the NFL didn't work, so it's hard to say anyone has a reason to sue. Still, despite all the ongoing debate over free speech, it's hard to deny the bulk of efforts to use government power to suppress political speech come not from the left, but the right.

All in all, Trump doesn't even really try to pretend that he believes that "free speech" is the right of conservatives to say offensive things without criticism or blowback from liberals. Consider the difference between his reaction to U.C. Berkeley shutting down a Milo Yiannopoulos speech (later rescheduled) for security reasons and his reaction to NBC News running stories that were critical of his presidency.

"If U.C. Berkeley does not allow free speech and practices violence on innocent people with a different point of view—NO

FEDERAL FUNDS?" Trump threatened on Twitter, after Yiannopoulos's speech was cancelled.

"With all of the Fake News coming out of NBC and the Networks, at what point is it appropriate to challenge their License? Bad for country!" Trump threatened after NBC News reported on some stupid things he said during a foreign policy meeting. He then kept at it, threatening the licenses of any network whose criticism he disliked.

Either way, Trump is threatening to use government force to control anyone who resists his agenda. But even the pretense that "free speech" is a thing he cares about, or even understands, has evaporated.

Trump and his supporters are not the carefree champions of gloves-off discourse, trying to loosen the overly tight strictures on political speech. They are the first to fly into offense at the slightest of challenges to white supremacy or to demand material penalties for disagreement with Trump's agenda. They are authoritarian bullies who cannot truck with disagreement. Their claims to be champions of "free speech" do not deserve to be taken seriously, ever again.

As for James Damore, the Google douchebag-cum-hero to the right: Was there any doubt this story ends with egg on the faces of his defenders? In late September, Damore, perhaps emboldened by the right giving him the status of a hero who speaks uncomfortable truths (never mind that they're not true), let loose with a truly stunning series of thoughts on Twitter:

"The KKK is horrible and I don't support them in any way, but can we admit that their internal names are cool e.g. 'Grand Wizard,'" the tweetstorm began.

"You know you've moralized an issue when you can't criticize its heroes or acknowledge any positive aspects of its villains," he continued, absolutely certain that others would see the value in not "moralizing" white supremacist terrorist organizations.

"It's like teaching your children to be responsible with drugs or sex without acknowledging that they can be fun," he continued, bringing up the question of how he came to believe there's a "responsible" way to engage in white supremacy. It's not like there's a condom that prevents you from catching racism when you strap on the white hood and demand an end to race-mixing.

"If they make the actual KKK the only place where you can acknowledge the coolness of D&D terms, then you'll just push people into the KKK," Damore ended.

(As an aside: What decade is Damore living in? The Lord of the Rings series was a massive hit 17 years ago. *Game of Thrones* is the most popular TV show in the world. Medieval fantasy is mainstream. Whatever is going on with Damore, he can't reasonably pretend that his enthusiasm for wizards and elves are why people don't like him.)

Damore swiftly deleted his bizarre defense of the apparent-only-to-him appeal of the KKK when he realized it was less popular than his women-are-dumb remarks from before. It was a strange move for a self-appointed champion of free speech who believes that our collective failure to make more room for reactionary arguments is undermining our commitment to robust public discourse. Nor was there a vigorous defense of him on the right. Apparently, there *is* a point where a right wing argument is so stupid that conservatives won't pretend that disagreement equals censorship.

Case Study: Stephen Miller

Stephen Miller, a thirty-something senior policy advisor for Donald Trump, is a noxious reactionary who gets off on trolling the more decent-minded—so much so that there's a pocket industry in mainstream journalism of stories about his youthful exploits that never really read quite as scandalous as he hoped.

There's the story about him telling a Latino friend that his ethnicity meant they could no longer be buddies. Or the speech he gave in high school declaring that students should not pick up their own lunch trash when there are janitors around to do it. Or how he wrote an op-ed in the school paper defending the genocide of Native Americans.

But my personal favorite is a story recounted in a *New York Times* profile written by Matt Flegenheimer: "He jumped, uninvited, into the final stretch of a girls' track meet, apparently intent on proving his athletic supremacy over the opposite sex."

Miller failed to make the point about female inferiority he was trying to make. Instead, he inadvertently created the perfect metaphor for male privilege: Let women do all the work, and then jump in at the very last minute to take all the credit.

With all the journalistic investigations into Miller, the one thing no one has yet to find out about the man is what, exactly, qualifies him to be a policy advisor. He leveraged an adolescence as a right wing troll—first at his California high school and then as a member of Duke University conservative groups—into a career not in policy, but in communications, working for the biggest loons in the Republican party.

"His passion for American exceptionalism and racial superiority eventually led him to jobs in Washington, D.C., first as a spokesperson for two right-wing members of Congress, Michele Bachmann and John Shadegg, and then as a policy adviser and communications director for conservative Alabama senator Jeff Sessions, now the U.S. attorney general," William Cohan of *Vanity Fair* wrote.

Miller then went on to help elect Republican congressman Dave Brat to office in Virginia, which required beating then-House majority leader Eric Cantor in the Republican primary. Miller's campaign work was fueled by a single-minded obsession with keeping non-white immigrants from moving to the United States.

It's arguable that Miller did more that almost any other person besides Trump to make immigration, which most Americans previously didn't have particularly strong opinions about, into a major issue that moves elections. The Brat campaign, for instance, was going nowhere until Brat started demagoguing about immigration, a move that likely had Miller's hand in it.

Miller no doubt has a talent for provoking the most racist instincts in the average Republican voter, but that loathing for people of color that moves him does not, it seems, translate well into competent policy-making. It was widely reported that Miller was the author of Trump's first attempt at a Muslim travel ban, and the policy was as badly designed as it was grossly bigoted. It took no time at all for courts to strike it down, and Miller was excised from later attempts to rewrite the travel ban to get it past the constitutional tests that the first ban clearly failed. But even though the administration got a little craftier about trying to make the Muslim ban seem a little less like a Muslim ban, judges continue to point to the original, Miller-penned Muslim ban as evidence of the original bigoted intent.

In nearly every picture of Miller, he looks like a man readying himself to snatch a canary out of a cage and stuff the still-living bird into his mouth to be swallowed whole. In his public appearances, he speaks with dripping condescension that indicates he believes the rest of the world to be little more than dog shit to be scraped off his shoe.

And if that sounds mean, well, dear reader, I wouldn't worry about it. On the contrary, I suspect if Miller ever reads this passage, he will take it as a compliment.

A top tier troll like Miller tends to relish the idea of being the villain. Being the bully who kicks sand in people's faces before spitting on them and calling them a "snowflake" is, in this day and age, seen as a role to aspire to for many on the right.

Miller's own personal affect fits very much into an alt-right aesthetic of gleeful villainy. In August, Miller took to the podium in the White House press room to defend Trump's immigration proposal, which was clearly based on policy ideas crafted by racist groups like the Federation for American Immigration Reform, which opposes a 1965 law that opened up immigration opportunities to people from non-European countries. Miller's demeanor during this presser recalled that of a Nazi officer in an Indiana Jones movie, as he stared down the journalists in the room with dead-eyed contempt.

One reporter, Jim Acosta on CNN, got confrontational with Miller and asked how the administration squares their anti-immigrant attitudes with the poem inscribed on the Statue of Liberty which reads, "Give me your tired, your poor, your huddled masses, yearning to breathe free."

"The poem that you're referring to was added later," Miller, whose first words as a child were no doubt, "um, actually," sneeringly replied.

The poem "is not actually part of the original Statue of Liberty," he added.

The comment was textbook bullshit. It's technically true that the poem was added 17 years after the statue was built, but Miller's insinuation—that it's silly to see the Statue of Liberty as a symbol of openness and welcome—makes no sense at all. The poem in question, "The New Colossus" by Emma Lazarus, was written to help fundraise to build the statue, and its location next to Ellis Island has made the statue history's most iconic symbol of the experience of immigration.

Miller then scornfully accused Acosta of being "cosmopolitan," which is the sort of thing white nationalists have thought of a sick burn dating all the way back to the literal Nazis.

The word choice, like much of Miller's behavior, is so on-the-nose and overwrought that it feels like a performance, as if he is someone who just watched a lot of WWII movies and thought it would be fun to play-act being a Nazi. This is something he has in common with the alt-right trolls that congregate online and, increasingly, at real life events like the Charlottesville rally. There's a very theatrical quality to all the diabolical posturing.

David Futrelle is a blogger who tracks online hate movements, such as the "men's rights" movement, Gamergate, and the burgeoning online fascist movement. As early as 2014, he noted that the alt-right types "*really* seem to enjoy depicting themselves as cartoon villains." They frequently decorate their websites and social media feeds with villainous imagery, such as "evil skulls with creepy eyes," and they frequently "identify themselves with fictional villains," such as Walter White from "Breaking Bad" or the Joker.

Since Futrelle wrote this, the tendency of alt-righters to deliberately portray themselves as villains has only gotten worse. Many identify as "shitlords" and they frequently make references to the human rights violations of fascists. There's a special love of portraying themselves pushing liberals out of helicopters, as Augusto Pinochet was reported doing to his political enemies. It's all a performance meant to scare people, especially the liberals so often deemed "snowflakes" and "cucks."

It's tempting to write these fools off as a bunch of sad sacks who resort to cheap shock value because they can't get attention any other way. And no doubt, that's a huge part of what drives the Stephen Millers of the world to run to the nearest microphone to say something nasty and racist in front of a crowd. But just because they are trolling for attention and outrage doesn't mean they don't mean the terrible things they say—or that they won't take action.

After all, Miller is in the White House, and however bad he is at it, he *is* writing policy. He likes scandalizing liberals with his showy performances of racism. But he also *is* a bigot, very sincerely so, and is doing everything he can to enshrine his vile ideas into law.

Chapter 3

Women

"Will the women's protest be over in time for them to cook dinner?"

So asked Republican Freeholder John Carman from Atlantic County, New Jersey, in response to the Women's March, the biggest single day protest—conservative estimates suggest more than 1 in every 100 Americans marched that day to protest Trump's inauguration—in the history of the country.

People marched for many reasons that day, but, as someone who was on the ground for the D.C. march, I can safely say that the biggest unifying point of anger was sexual violence. Trump is a confessed sexual predator who bragged that he likes to "grab 'em by the pussy" on a hot mic, and his election was a searing hot reminder to women across the country of how little we are valued as human beings, and how traumatic that can often be.

So naturally, troll nation has to make jokes like Carman's, the point of which is, like all sexist jokes, that women aren't really people and women would be fools to think otherwise. We're dinner-makers and sex toys and toilet scrubbers and patient distributors of flattery to the male ego, but we must never, ever think we are people. And if we start to think that, troll nation will get the ultimate revenge by electing to the presidency a sexual predator who treats women like disposable rags. Just to remind us of our place.

But reminding women of their place is an endless task, one that never stops for vacations or inaugurations. So it was that these tired, sexist jokes in response to the Women's March were sadly common.

Nebraska state senator Bill Kintor tweeted a photo of three women holding up signs denouncing sexual assault with the caption, "Ladies, I think you're safe." Women are meant to see rape as flattery, it seems.

Erick Erickson, a conservative commentator who has been published by the *New York Times* tweeted, "I feel sorry for all the ham and cheese that won't get made into sandwiches while all those women are marching."

(Leave it to a right wing man to underestimate the female ability to get shit done while also fighting to save the world. My friend's mother made sure that a small army of friends and family members went into that protest with a healthy box lunch in hand.)

A New Mexico city councilor named J. R. Doporto wrote on Facebook, "stop your bitching" and "you also have the right to be slapped."

TV host Piers Morgan whined about the "creeping global emasculation" that he believed the march represented.

"What MORE do you want? Free mani/pedis?" tweeted Michael Flynn Jr., whose father had been appointed to the White

House staff. (Answer: To begin with, not electing sexual predators to the White House.)

"My shirts aren't going to iron themselves," tweeted talk radio host John Cardillo.

Sean Todd, a town councilor from Rhode Island, tweeted, "Definitely a guy came up with the idea for the #womensmarch perfect way to get the wives outta the house."

(Women definitely cannot be allowed credit for their ideas.)

Infowars host Alex Jones called the marchers "unattractive troll-like women."

"Overweight homely women march in DC with 'pussy grab' pink hats," tweeted Jim Hoft, a blogger the Trump White House gave press credentials to. (While there, he took a photo of himself flashing a white supremacist symbol at the press secretary's podium.)

Gender is the only issue that's up there with race that had done more to excite, and frankly form, troll nation. It really shouldn't be a surprise. Backlashes follow feminist gains as surely as night follows day. The idea of women's equality is particularly unsettling to a certain kind of mediocre man—like Trump or any of the authors of these unfunny jokes—who knows that without the artificial lift that male privilege gives him in the world, everyone would easily see that he is undeserving of any plum jobs or positions. So these men lash out, clinging to the power that was unfairly given them in the first place, and undermining any progress feminists make.

Women's gains in the '40s were notoriously met with a huge backlash in the '50s, when so many women were unceremoniously shoved back into the home after working in paid jobs during the war. It happened again in the '80s, when the dramatic gains of the '70s ended in the Reagan Revolution. The '90s had a small feminist moment, with Anita Hill and Riot Grrrl, and that was set aflame by the surge in the early 2000s of religious right misogyny, epitomized by George W. Bush and his administration's "abstinence-only" agenda.

And so it's not a surprise, really, to see it happening again. But it feels different this time, for a number of reasons. For one thing, it really does feel like it's less cyclical and more simultaneous. The Women's March made it clear that the backlash isn't going to cause women to tone it down and retreat into the shadows. But I also think the nature of the argument about women's rights and women's roles has changed in significant ways from the debates that happened before.

This time, the backlash isn't coming from traditionalists trying to make substantive arguments, so much as it's coming from troll nation. The backlash is fewer Bible verses and scare stories about how no one will love you if you don't marry by 40, and more make-me-a-sandwich jokes. While sexists can still be seen doing that thing where they pretend they have substantive claims and may even pretend they care about women, it's not a strategy that has as much traction as it used to. The backlash these days is rawer, less apologetic, and more openly misogynist than it felt in the past.

I lived through the last backlash, when George W. Bush was elected, and so I'd like to think I have some frame of reference. Back in the ancient days of the early 2000s, the He Man Woman Haters Club was just as irritating, but in a different way: Smug and sanctimonious, clutching their Bibles to their chests and swearing up and down that they want to take rights away to *help* the little ladies. Bush himself was pretty good at the weepy-eyed bullshit, often getting so sentimental about the fates of aborted embryos that he actually fooled some people into thinking he actually thought "pro-life" was a thing, instead of a cheap political gambit to strip away women's rights.

During the Bush years, the anti-feminist right's strategy was to portray feminism as some kind of well-intended mistake that had done more harm than good, and to argue that women had to be rescued from having rights for their own sake. Mostly, the fight focused on women's sexual autonomy.

For those who were too young to remember those days, it's probably hard to believe how silly the antagonism towards women's rights and sexuality got. It was so bad that poor Britney Spears seems to have been under some contractual obligation to pretend she was a virgin, even as she sang cheerfully lewd pop songs. (Pop songs *should* be lewd. But pop singers should not feel like they have to perform virginity for some leering old sexists while singing sexy tunes.) Abstinence-only became this bizarre teen trend, with kids being pressured into public ceremonies where they vowed chastity until marriage and even got rings inscribed with their virginity pledges. Books and blogs about waiting for marriage—or regretting not waiting for marriage—became popular.

The Republicans backed all this up with policy. The war on abortion rights expanded to become a war on contraception, though then, as now, it's really hard to get conservatives to admit to what they're up to. (Makes sense, as 99 percent of sexually active women have used birth control, which is a sobering statistic for anyone trying to demonize the practice.) The Bush administration aggressively pushed abstinence-only and fought efforts to improve contraception access, as well.

The argument back then always came back to this notion that feminism and sexual liberation were bad for women. There were both religious and pseudo-scientific claims that women who had sexual partners before marriage became unlovable and destined for a future surrounded by cats dressed in baby clothes. One Bush appointee to Health and Human Services even tried to argue that hormones released during premarital sex burned out women's brains and made them unable to pair-bond with a future husband.

The ruse of feigned concern for women worked for a time, but it collapsed by the time Barack Obama was elected. Part of it, I think, was that the internet gave women, especially young women, a way to talk back to this paternalistic garbage. Feminist blogs both small and mighty made daily sport out of mocking the Bible-clutching faux solictude for wayward women. This insolent feminist tone started leaking into the mainstream media. The organized feminist movement deserves a lot of credit as well for doing the heavy lifting of providing the research and analysis showing, indisputably, that women are better off when they have access to reproductive health care and the right to make their own decisions. Democrats fully embraced feminism, making women's rights the center of their campaign strategies.

I'd argue that, when it comes to reasoned discourse, feminists largely won the public argument. Nowadays, mainstream media sources largely treat it as self-evident that the gender inequality is a problem, sexual harassment and abuse is wrong, and reproductive health care improves women's health. Conservatives still make bad faith arguments where they pretend to be so worried that feminism hurts women—Ross Douthat of the *New York Times* is always reliable on this front—but the will to keep up the sham seems to have faded dramatically since the Bush years.

Into this void rushed troll nation, which does not bother to pretend to care about women and mostly wishes to snicker at how clever it is to tweet "make me a sandwich" at feminists for the 15th million time.

The internet played a huge role in the rise of 21st century feminism, and unfortunately, it's doing the same for this new breed of anti-feminism that doesn't even pretend to be anything but a rage wind blown by bitter men. The internet is a rat's nest of "men's rights activists," most of whom mistake trolling and shit-talking women for activism. Many of them also identify as "pickup artists" or "red-pill," and dedicate themselves to the fantasy that the way to get laid is to treat women like shit—though, reading their forums, it becomes clear that treating women like shit is far more the draw than sex ever could be. Gamergate became its own little subculture on the internet, eventually spawning a generation of youthful Trump fans and white supremacists.

Journalists noticed these wretched specimens in the years before the 2016 election, of course. It was hard not to, as they tended to swarm like cockroaches on social media and comment sections of web publications.

But it was widely believed, even among many feminists, that these jackasses were a small, if loud, percentage of the population. It was easy to imagine them as sweaty, basement-dwelling losers. Most of us didn't want to believe the guy ranting online about how feminists are all hairy bitches who scream rape at the drop of a hat could be the ordinary married guy living next door.

The election of Trump—whose own Twitter feed is indistinguishable from the typical "men's rights activist"—stripped away that illusion. The raving woman-hating creep was everywhere. He's the president. He's your neighbor. He's the guy playing against you in an online video game. He's the millions of men who voted for Trump. The reason those guys seem everywhere online is because they are everywhere, period. They are legion.

To be clear, the Bible-hugging misogynists are still with us. (See: Pence, Mike.) But woman-haters have been freed. They don't have to pretend that this is about god or tradition or family anymore. "Fuck you, bitch, make me a sandwich" is the unofficial motto that rides sidecar to "Make America great again."

At the Republican National Convention in 2016, there was so much grotesque misogyny on display that a number of journalists in Cleveland to cover the convention seemed downright traumatized by it. "Hillary sucks, but not like Monica" shirts were selling at a brisk pace and visible all over the city. "Trump that bitch!" was another popular slogan, as were buttons and T-shirts shaming Hillary Clinton for her body. Also popular were T-shirts and signs that showed Trump enacting physical violence of some sort on Clinton.

But this sort of misogyny wasn't just part of the unofficial celebrations. Multiple speakers, especially Gov. Chris Christie of New Jersey and Lt. Gen. Michael Flynn, portrayed Clinton—without any evidence whatsoever—as a criminal, leading the crowd repeatedly in bloodthirsty chants of, "Lock her up! Lock her up!"

In his speech, Ben Carson even implied that Clinton worships Satan. In college, Clinton wrote a paper about the '60s-era organizer Saul Alinsky. In his speech, Carson warned that Alinsky "acknowledges Lucifer, the original radical who gained his own kingdom."

(Alinsky makes a literary reference to Lucifer in his book *Rules for Radicals*, which right wing mythmakers have massaged into false accusations of devil worship. In reality, it's highly doubtful that Alinsky, unlike Carson, even believed in a literal devil.)

"So are we willing to elect someone as president who has as their role model somebody who acknowledges Lucifer?" Carson asked. "Think about that."

Hmmm, deep.

Sitting in the stands, it was clear to me that the "crime" that so offended the chanters, who the volume indicated were most of the delegates at the convention, was not actually any specific law-breaking. Or devil worship. No, Clinton was clearly seen as out of order for being a woman with ambition, and that was why the crowds wanted to see her locked up.

"Since Goody Rodham was placed in the water and thence did float & was observed conversing with a tall man in the woods, is she not GUILTY?" tweeted journalist Rebecca Traister.

The in-your-face misogyny on display at the Republican National Convention, while disturbing for those of us who were there to cover it, really shouldn't have been surprising. Shit, as they say, rolls downhill, and the newly anointed head of the party, Trump, is himself a sleazy woman-hater of the first order.

"Such a nasty woman," Trump famously snarled during the third presidential debate with Clinton.

It was already well-established at that point that Clinton, just by being a woman who is not hired eye candy, deeply unsettled Trump. During the second debate, he stalked around stage, sometimes staring at Clinton's body in a deeply weird way and sometimes lurking around behind her threateningly. Still, his calling her a "nasty woman" still was a massive WTF moment because, right then, she was literally talking about the driest subject imaginable, Social Security taxes.

"I am on record as saying we need to put more money into the Social Security trust fund," she said. "That's part of my commitment to raise taxes on the wealthy. My Social Security payroll contribution will go up as will Donald's, assuming he can't figure out how to get out of it, but what we want to do is—"

At this point, Trump spewed his "nasty woman" comment. Granted, it was more a response to Clinton taking a potshot over an issue her campaign had repeatedly raised—Trump's unprecedented unwillingness to release his tax returns—but little jabs over actual campaign issues is par for the course in modern politics. Just straight up freaking out on a woman because she doesn't fit your '50s-era ideal of womanhood, however, is not something people do these days. Or it wasn't, until Trump came leering onto the scene.

It was one of many, many moments that felt like a tipping point that would cause voters to wake up to the realities of electing someone who sees half the human race, including his own daughter, as sex objects who have no purpose in existing after their tits have given into gravity. Instead, what we learned is no, Trump's voters either accept that's just how men think or they openly like it. After all, these are the same people chanting "lock her up." Sexism is far more deeply embedded in American culture than many of us wanted to believe.

And really, Trump's attitudes towards women were not hidden by the time he was leering and fulminating at Clinton during the debates. During the campaign season alone, he called Fox News anchor Megyn Kelly a "bimbo" and made a joke about her being on her period after she asked a confrontational question during a Republican primary debate. He also insulted Republican primary candidate Carly Fiorina by saying, "Look at that face! Would anyone vote for that?" Upon finding out that Clinton had to use the bathroom during the break of a Democratic primary debate—and Trump has repeatedly made it clear he does not approve of women having body functions—he mocked her for it, calling her "disgusting."

Before that, Trump literally built his tabloid-bait-style brand by being a caricature of a rich misogynist who treats women like trash. The listicles put together of vicious things Trump has said about women, of which there are many online, are deadening in their length and volume. When he spoke about women in public, Trump almost always focused on their looks and on ranking them on his ever-present hot-or-not scale. This includes his daughter Ivanka, whose body he has publicly drooled over since she was a teenager and who he repeatedly indicated he would like to date, if not for that pesky incest taboo.

Troll nation, however, sees this behavior towards women and interprets it in a positive light: hey, at least he's being honest. For it is widely believed in troll nation that all men, everywhere, hold women in contempt, and the only difference is some men admit it and some pretend not to. That's why men who express feminist ideas are so frequently accused of "virtue-signaling." The idea that such sentiments could be sincere is preposterous to many on the right.

This context sheds light on why it is that a tape of Trump bragging to *Access Hollywood* host Billy Bush about how he sexually assaults women, caught by producers on a hot mic, did not have the effect on Republican voters that many liberals thought it would.

Sexual harassment and the kind of abuse that Trump bragged about, at its core, is a form of trolling. The harasser's goal is to make a woman uncomfortable. The thrill is in lording your power over a woman. Grabbing a woman's ass in a crowded elevator isn't most people's idea of a deeply satisfying sexual experience, after all. The point of it is relishing the power to make her unhappy and in knowing she can't do anything about it.

Trump himself made this clear on the tape.

"When you're a star, they let you do it," he gloated. "Grab them by the pussy. You can do anything."

Sexual harassment, like overt racism, is one of those forms of trolling and bullying that exists in a gray area for conservatives. On one hand, it's so obviously cruel and often criminal that most conservatives, at least those who aren't Milo Yiannopoulos, won't outright endorse it. On the other hand, it was clear that most of them just don't really take it seriously and thought that liberal outrage at Trump was being faked for partisan purposes.

"Enough of the fake outrage," one female Trump supporter wrote on his Facebook page. "If American women are so outraged at Trump's use of naughty words, then who the hell bought 80 million copies of *Fifty Shades of Grey*?"

(Apparently, if you like to read erotic fiction about consensual BDSM with a super hot guy, you are obligated to let some gross old pervert grab your pussy while crowing about how you can't stop him.)

"Every guy in the United States of America has talked about doing a girl," a female Trump supporter told *Mother Jones*. "In the bathroom. Or in the locker room, or wherever—on the bus."

Of course, Trump wasn't talking about "doing a girl." He was talking about forcing himself on women whose very lack of interest made it fun for him.

"There's a lot of people in Hollywood, a lot of music people, rappers, that say a lot more dangerous and nasty language," another woman said defensively.

Of course, writing it off as just words fails to account for the more than a dozen women who have described being assaulted by Trump in exactly the manner he describes.

The fact that right wing America doesn't actually consider sexual harassment a real problem, but instead just as a cheap partisan shot, was evident in the reaction to the accusations that came out in the fall of 2017 against Hollywood mogul Harvey Weinstein. The same right wing media that downplayed allegations against Trump and covered up similar allegations against Fox News host Roger Ailes and Fox News host Bill O'Reilly suddenly discovered their ability to feel outrage at sexual abuse. But that's because Weinstein is a Democratic donor, not because sexual harassment is actually foul behavior in their eyes. While accusations against O'Reilly, Ailes, and Trump got minimal coverage on Fox News, the Weinstein story got 24/7 coverage for weeks.

Yep, that's how low the 21st century conservative movement will go: sexual harassment holds no interest for them, unless it can be used to troll liberals. Otherwise, they don't give a single flying fuck—and in fact, can't wait to vote for an admitted sexual assailant for president.

Trump's personal misogyny is backed up by sexist policy. Despite his long history of desperately trying, and failing, to convince the press of his sexual magnetism (tabloid reporters understood that Trump's access to women was more about his money than his charm), Trump as president embraced sexual health policies that were categorically anti-sex, at least for women. His policies on abortion, contraception and sex education are based on the notion that women should only have sex for the purposes of procreation—and that women who have sex for pleasure are dirty sluts who should be punished.

It's not just that Trump the politician fully committed to an anti-abortion stance, while refusing to answer Maureen Dowd when she asked if he had ever paid for an abortion during his pre-politics days. (He did publicly hint back then that he tried to talk his second wife, Marla Maples, into terminating a pregnancy.) Despite his own sexual history, the Trump administration took the anti-abortion, anti-contraception stance of the Bush administration and doubled down on it.

Teresa Manning, Trump's pick to run the federal program helping low income women access birth control, had previously given an interview to NPR where she said, "Contraception doesn't work. Its efficacy is very low."

"In fact, the incidence of contraception use and the incidence of abortion go up hand in hand," she added.

(This idea that contraception causes abortion is a common theory in religious right circles. They argue that if people don't have contraception, they will choose abstinence, and therefore will have fewer abortions. In reality, repeated research links high abortion rates to poor access to contraception. This makes sense, as the most popular contraception methods work 82 percent–99.5 percent of the time, whereas using no contraception means there's an 85 percent chance of pregnancy in a year. That, and most people like fucking too much to just give it up.)

Another pick of Trump's to help on health care policy, Katy Talento, repeatedly argued that birth control pills are really abortion and that using them will break "your uterus for good."

These views ended up in a White House memo, leaked to

Crooked Media in 2017, that outlined the Trump administration's budget goals. The memo recommended completely zeroing out all funding for teen pregnancy prevention programs, and replacing them with "fertility awareness methods," which is jargon for the rhythm method. Yes, they really proposed that teen girls should track their periods and schedule sex for times of the month that they were unlikely to be ovulating, rather than rely on simple methods like condoms or pills.

In all honesty, though, the likelier explanation is Trump's team just wants teen girls to get pregnant. After all, there's nothing like a pregnant belly to let you know which girls in your community are having sex. It just really simplifies the process of shaming and shunning them.

Trump's hostility towards women, especially young women, was also expressed by the administration's approach to sexual violence. Betsy DeVos, after Trump appointed her to head the Department of Education, immediately set to work reversing Obama-era recommendations to fight sexual violence at universities. Previously, the Education Department under Obama had suggested to universities that they use the same legal standard in settling sexual assault accusations against students that courts use to determine guilt in civil courts. DeVos, on the other hand, recommended a higher standard than the one used in civil courts—therefore making it harder for a school to punish a student for rape than for other crimes against fellow students, such as theft or non-sexual assault.

Candice Jackson, who was hired by DeVos to head up the civil rights division at the Education Department, accused the vast majority of rape victims of lying.

"The accusations—90 percent of them—fall into the category

of 'we were both drunk,' 'we broke up, and six months later I found myself under a Title IX investigation because she just decided that our last [time] sleeping together was not quite right,'" she told the *New York Times*.

In reality, FBI statistics show that 2–8 percent of rape reports are wrong. The percentage of false *accusations*, however, is even smaller. The typical false reporter is seeking attention and sympathy, and doesn't want to get anyone in trouble. Most tend to make up a stranger jumping out of the bushes, instead of accusing men they actually know.

But is it any surprise that the Trump administration has a strong interest in portraying rape victims as lying sluts and making it much harder for victims to get justice? Trump himself has a clear personal interest in reinstating the widespread social belief that women who are assaulted were asking for it.

Being soft on rape and hostile to contraception should, by any measure, be bad politics. It speaks to the belligerence of troll nation, however, that Republicans continue to win with policies that not only dehumanize half the population, but that put great stress on the families and spouses of women who need to be safe, productive, and able to avoid having more children than they can reasonably house and feed.

Right wing media has a nifty way to distract conservatives from the material effects of anti-woman policies, however: make the entire issue about trolling feminists, who are portrayed alternately as ball-busting hags or too-sexy bitches who need to be taken down a peg.

Rush Limbaugh, for instance, effectively turned his right wing audiences against a federal rule requiring insurance companies to cover contraception by attacking Sandra Fluke, a Georgetown law student who testified at a congressional hearing in favor of the policy. Over the course of three days in 2012, Limbaugh lobbed 46 insults at Fluke, suggesting that she is a prostitute and calling her a "slut" for her belief that contraception is a normal part of women's health care.

"A Georgetown co-ed told Rep. Nancy Pelosi's hearing that the women in her law school program are having so much sex that they're going broke, so you and I should pay for their birth control," he ranted.

"She's having so much sex she can't afford the contraception," he continued, seemingly unaware that the number of birth control pills a woman takes does not correlate with the amount of sex she has.

"I will buy all of the women at Georgetown University as much aspirin to put between their knees as they want," he sneered.

Limbaugh's strategy here wasn't particularly subtle. He set up Fluke, and other "co-eds" as these crazy party girls who are having all this fun sex—and insinuated that his listeners should be jealous and resentful.

"Ms. Fluke and the rest of you feminazis, here's the deal," he whined. "We want you to post the videos online [of them having sex] so we can all watch."

Having secured the image of feminists as oversexed hotties who are excluding you, Joe Conservative, from all the fun, it's easy for Limbaugh to then sell anti-contraception policies as a way to get revenge. If those women want to have all that sexy sex without sharing it with you, he intimates, well, you can at least punish them with an unwanted pregnancy.

Tucker Carlson of Fox News plays this game frequently, as well. A favorite target of his is Lauren Duca, a *Teen Vogue* writer whose political writings for her young, fashion-oriented audience have drawn Carlson's ire. Duca is young, smart, and pretty, and so is a perfect hate object to provoke sexist male resentment, both of the sexual variety and because they're annoyed that a young woman is being treated as intelligent and important in mainstream media.

"You should stick to the thigh-high boots, you're better at that," Carlson snarled at Duca when she dared criticize Trump for his sexism.

In other segments, he has called her "vapid," "frothy" and says she can "barely write." It's all nonsense, but it's what his audience wants to hear: that a pretty young woman's only purpose is to be a mindless sex object, and if a woman rejects that role, she deserves to be browbeaten and bullied.

The whole thing really exposes the toxic thinking that has created our current political moment. Conservative audiences have been repeatedly encouraged to be resentful, and to take all the normal dissatisfactions of everyday life and channel that frustration into hurting liberals, even if doing so comes at great cost to themselves. Shaming women for having sex or hounding them out of their jobs will hurt the sex lives and pocketbooks of right wing America, too. But sadly, too many of them see that as a reasonable price to pay to make the feminists suffer.

Case Study: Roy Moore

The rule of thumb to determine who Republicans, especially the base voters, will support in the age of Trump is quite simple: whoever they believe will annoy liberals the most will get their vote. It's that impulse that helped Trump win a whopping 37 out of 50 states in the Republican primary. It's why the only two other primary candidates that were ever even slightly competitive against Trump in the primary, Ted Cruz and Ben Carson, also happened to be the two who espoused the kookiest, and thus most liberal-annoying, views.

When "suck it, libtards" is your primary motivation for voting, then the quickest way to aggravate them is to go for the guy who most makes liberals worryingly imagine a post-apocalyptic disaster scenario.

The exact flavor of the apocalypse doesn't matter that much, so long as liberals are worried about it. Trump himself invokes legitimate fears of both a Pinochet-style fascist state and fears that we're all going to die in a nuclear war. Either scenario makes liberals sweat, and so causes glee on the right, even though conservatives should rationally reconsider whether they'd really thrive in a Trump-caused nuclear wasteland any better than the loathed liberals.

The Alabama special election, meant to fill the Senate seat that was vacated when Jeff Sessions joined the Trump administration as attorney general, demonstrated that a "Handmaid's Tale"-style theocratic dystopia is also acceptable to the right, so long as it causes liberals to lose sleep.

The political press closely watched the primary run-off for the Republican nominee for the Alabama senate seat, precisely because it was seen as an answer to the question of how nutty Republican voters were willing to go in their endless bid to troll the rest of the country. Both contenders, Roy Moore and Luther Strange, were far-right ideologues that portrayed themselves as Trump-like figures. But Strange was generally perceived as somewhat sane, which ended up working against him.

The sad thing is that the election wasn't even really close. Moore trounced Strange 55–45, a huge spread for a primary win against a candidate who has the party's backing.

The go-to word for Moore in the aftermath of the election was "firebrand," but a better adjective would have been "bugfuck." Moore has never overtly declared himself a member of the extremely far-right Christian Reconstruction movement, but most experts in right wing fringe movements have garnered, from his public statements and his frequent appearances at Reconstruction events that he, at minimum, has an affinity for this fringe-of-the-fringe theocratic movement.

"The long-term goal of Christians in politics should be to gain exclusive control over the franchise," wrote Christian Reconstructionist Gary North in his 1989 book *Political Polytheism: The Myth of Pluralism*, while adding that those "who refuse to submit publicly" should be denied the right to citizenship.

It's a theology and political philosophy that is also tied up in the grotesque racial politics of the far right. Moore has a habit of targeting black Americans with objections to their right to citizenship, objections tied into his own peculiar views on religion. He has gone beyond the "just asking questions" strategy that most birthers use to suggest that Barack Obama is not a natural-born citizen, and openly declared in 2016 that he does not believe Obama was born in the United States.

Moore also argued in 2006 that congressional representative Keith Ellison should not be allowed to serve in Congress, due to Ellison's Muslim faith. In the same editorial, he compared taking the oath with a Koran to be the equivalent to swearing on a copy of *Mein Kampf.*

Moore rejects the plain language reading of the Constitution, as well as Founder-penned supporting documents like the Federalist Papers, that make it clear that the United States was enshrined as a secular nation with freedom of religion. Instead, Moore argues, "God is the only source of our law, liberty and government."

This notion that the Founders really wanted a theocracy is a classic Reconstructionist idea that has, sadly, spread like a virus through the larger religious right. Believers, of course, offer some tortured justifications for why we should believe that the Founders intended this to be a theocratic nation, but as with their other cherished beliefs—evolution is a lie, climate change is a hoax, and Obama was born in Kenya—the reality is that it's just a bunch of wishful thinking, easily debunked.

What matters is that Moore uses these half-baked philosophies to justify repeated, illegal decisions that stemmed from his authoritarian disrespect for the rule of law and democratic systems. Twice he was removed from his position on the Alabama Supreme Court, because he argued that his interpretation of the Bible should trump the actual law of the land.

In 2003, Moore rejected the constitutional injunction against establishment of religion by refusing to remove an enormous granite statue of the Ten Commandments from the lobby of the state courthouse. He managed to worm his way back into power, and lost it again in 2016 when he tried to prevent same-sex marriage from being enacted in Alabama, despite a Supreme Court ruling that legalized it in all 50 states.

His racism is so over-the-top that it's cartoonish. During the campaign, he literally called Native Americans and Asian Americans "reds and yellows." His homophobia is just as virulent. In 2002, he wrote a court opinion calling same-sex relations "a crime against nature, an inherent evil, and an act so heinous that it defies one's ability to describe it."

(No one tell him that there's few, if any, sex acts that same-sex couples can do in bed that straight couples can't.)

I could go on and on, but it hardly matters. Moore makes Iranian ayatollahs recoil at his extremism. But right wing politics are defined these days by the principle that the biggest nut gets the trophy, and so Moore was a shoo-in for the Republican nominee—and since this is Alabama, also for the Senate.

It's not like Strange was falling down in the over-the-top-right-wing-nut department. Trump himself showed up in Alabama to stump for Strange. (Though there's a not-small chance that the only reason Trump picked Strange over Moore is that he was impressed by Strange's 6'9" stature.) But having Trump in your corner doesn't help, when the only thing that matters is which candidate causes liberals to panic the most.

Strange, being a Bible Belt politician, made sure to do a lot of heavy lifting for the anti-sex squad, such as suing the government in an effort to stop an HHS regulation requiring health insurance plans to cover contraception. But even that move against contraception access couldn't compete with Moore's views on the subject, since Moore cheerfully lambasted the Supreme Court for legalizing birth control in the first place.

It's that sort of thing that really drives home how much the choices being made by Republican voters have little relationship to any policy concerns or real life issues that affect them directly. Most Alabamians, like most Americans, use contraception. (Guttmacher research shows that 99 percent of women who have sex with men have used contraception.) It's quite unlikely that these voters actually want to see the birth control they rely on become illegal. And yet they vote, eagerly, for a man who loudly protests the court decision that allows them to access the contraception nearly all of them have used.

That disconnect between their policy positions and their own lived experiences defines the nature of the right wing troll mentality. When birth control is discussed in the political realm, it ceases to be a service that they themselves use on a regular basis, but instead becomes purely symbolic. The idea of making feminists cry by taking away their birth control pills is so delicious to conservatives that they end up conveniently forgetting that they use the exact same birth control pills for the exact same reasons as those hated feminists.

Steve Bannon, the fired White House chief strategist under Trump and former head of the right wing website Breitbart, was blunt about this view of Moore's usefulness as a candidate.

"It's a revolt against the elites in this country," Bannon said on the Breitbart show on Sirius XM. "It's a revolt against the globalists among those elites. It's a revolt against the progressive agenda that is trying to be jammed down the throat of the American people."

It's pretentious rhetoric, but the basic gist is simple enough. Bannon couldn't be bothered to even pretend to care about Moore's ideas or agenda. Moore is unfit for office, but that, if anything, recommends him to Bannon and the Breitbart audience.

Unfit for office is exactly the sort of thing that makes liberals perspire, and making liberals unhappy is the singular objective of troll nation.

Things took a bizarre turn in November 2017, a month before the election, when the *Washington Post* published a well-sourced expose of Moore's alleged history of chasing teen girls when he was in his '30s and working as an assistant district attorney in Etowah County, Alabama. The Post reporters spoke with four women who claimed he had a taste for the young ones and would use sleazy tactics—such as offering to babysit, cruising the high school, or hovering over girls at their jobs at the mall—to prey on high school girls. One girl was 14 when she said he picked her up in his car, stripped some of her clothes from her, and tried to get her to handle his penis.

Soon, more women stepped forward, with one woman alleging that, when she was 16 and he was 30, Moore had assaulted her in such a way that she feared he might rape her.

Troll nation didn't miss a beat or waste any time worrying about things like whether the accusations were true or disqualifying. Liberals clearly hate Moore, and hated him even more hearing these stories, and that was reason enough for many conservatives to support him. Breitbart swung into action, preemptively posting Moore's campaign rebuttal before the *Post* story went live. Joel Pollack, a Breitbart reporter, complained on MSNBC that the *Post* story contained "perfectly legitimate relationships as well as all kinds of other political clutter."

Moore and his cronies had a built-in narrative: who ya gonna believe, red state Bible-thumping white men or the liberal media? Moore and his supporters even started comparing his plight to the persecution of Jesus. Anti-abortion activists argued that

Moore was justified because "there is something about a purity of a young woman, there is something that is good, that's true, that's straight and he looked for that." The implication is that chasing teenagers, who are more likely to be virgins, was a religious choice—and that criticizing that was somehow oppressive to Moore's faith.

Meanwhile, Republican establishment types wanting to distance themselves from Moore, followed Senate Majority Leader Mitch McConnell when he said he believed the women. This, in turn, led the fiercest Trump loyalists to turn on McConnell and other Republicans. Expressing distaste for a man who was reportedly banned from the mall for creeping on teenage girls was enough to cause Trump lovers to declare Republicans "cucks" who were giving into liberal pressure. The most popular forum for Trump supporters on the internet, The Donald at Reddit, came alive with conspiracy theories claiming that the accusers were liars being paid off by Democrats and/or Republicans like McConnell who were supposedly afraid to Make America Great Again.

What makes the situation even weirder is that the self-proclaimed "edgelords" and Breitbart readers that make up Trump's most ardent fan base are men that, while clearly enamored of fascism, show very little interest in the pious Bible-clutching fundamentalism of Moore and his Bible Belt voters. These are men who are more likely to spend their time on "pick-up artist" websites than chatting about the value of premarital chastity. Many of them are far more interested in going out drinking on Saturday night and staying in Sunday to play video games than they are in attending Bible study and church services. Bannon himself is a known party animal who throws shindigs that last until the wee hours of the morning. If they gave it a single moment's thought, they probably wouldn't like living in a Christian theocracy that Moore promotes, no more than the feminists they hate so much would.

But the fierce tribalism of troll nation has terminated even the last remaining flickers of common sense. For the Bannon right, liberals are the enemy to be extinguished at all cost and mainstream Republicans, no matter how far they are to the right politically, are viewed as a bunch of pussies because they sometimes deign to act like they believe Democrats are human beings. Troll nation may not agree with Moore's flavor of radical right wing politics, but its members appreciate how nuts he is. And outrage over stories about him touching teenage girls is just more of that "political correctness" they want to stomp out.

Subsequently, Alabama's special election became a test of how much the trolling mentality had taken over the Republican Party. The state is solidly Republican, and outside of the cities, Democrats don't have a chance. But many liberals hoped that voters, when faced with a literal choice between an accused kiddie-grabber and a Democrat, would find it in their hearts to hate liberals less than they hate gross older men who think high school freshmen are "pure" enough to touch your penis.

The results were mixed. On one hand, 68 percent of white voters decided that an accused child molester was still better than one of those hated liberals. However, Democrats in Alabama, energized by both the anti-Trump resistance and the knowledge that their opponent was literally an accused child molester, turned out in droves to vote, pushing Doug Jones over the top.

The lesson is simple: There is no such thing as shame or moral boundaries for troll nation. But they can be outvoted, if liberals are willing to actually turn up at the polls.

Chapter 4

The Environment

The extent to which right wing politics is shaped mainly, sometimes exclusively, by an urge to troll the left is played out, perhaps mostly alarmingly, on the issue of the environment.

At first blush, this might seem ridiculous. How is it that the human impacts on air, water, biodiversity, and climate patterns are being controlled by the tedious culture war politics perpetuated by the right? Could it really be possible that the fate of the planet is being distorted by that craven right wing impulse to stick it to the liberals?

In fact, there's good reason to believe the right wing agenda on the environment, especially in the age of Trump, is guided mainly by figuring out whatever it is that liberals care about, and trying to destroy it. Corporate profits do play a role, to be clear, but it's increasingly clear that huge chunks of the right wing agenda on the environment have nothing to do with the venial impulses of capitalists. It's about hating liberals.

An early sign from the people that are gently called "the base" in the media was a trend deemed "rolling coal." It's a practice that requires modifying a diesel engine, usually in a pick-up truck, so that the driver can dump a bunch of fuel into the engine, emitting a big plume of sooty black smoke. Some truck owners also add smokestacks to add to the effect.

While the practice started in truck-pull contests as a way to add drama to the proceedings, it's since morphed into a bizarre political practice. YouTube is rife with videos of motorists shooting plumes of diesel smoke at anyone they perceive as liberal.

At first, rolling coal was done mainly to taunt people driving electric or hybrid cars, or maybe bicyclists—anyone viewed as caring about the problem of climate change, and therefore hated for it. Then the practice expanded. Now many of the most popular videos show drivers rolling coal on Black Lives Matter or anti-Trump protesters.

What's interesting about rolling coal as a practice is that it has no value outside of trolling liberals. In fact, it costs the coal-roller a pretty penny, since modifying trucks to do this can cost hundreds, even thousands of dollars. Plus, dumping extra fuel in your engine adds to the gas bill. It's also illegal in many states, which means that the person who does it is risking a fine.

It's an expensive way for conservatives to take an issue that should be about science and the self-preservation of the human race, and rewriting it to be an issue of tribal identity politics. Serious questions about the future of our planet are reduced to identity markers. The choice between caring about climate change vs. denying it's real is treated as no different than the choice between liking country western vs. liking hip-hop, or drinking domestic beer vs. drinking fancy imports.

This could be more easily shrugged off, but the tendency to spin environmental issues as culture war politics has reached the highest levels of politics, controlling political choices in both Congress and the White House.

Climate change denialism started as a way to pander to oil companies, no doubt. Republican politicians were and still are afraid to say out loud that they believe climate change is real and human-caused, for fear of upsetting their billionaire oilmen benefactors. But nowadays, companies like ExxonMobil, Chevron, and Shell have publicly admitted that human-caused climate change is real, even if they're only doing so in service of a public relations strategy. But Republican politicians still dodge and weave or even outright deny when asked about climate change.

The reason is that they're afraid of their voters. Climate change has become a culture war issue, and admitting it is real is viewed as tantamount to letting liberals win. And that cannot happen, even if the cost is the destruction of the planet that the children born from all those traditional family values are supposed to inherit. Republicans need those coal-rollers to win, so they continue to pretend not to realize that there's a multi-decade scientific consensus around the question of whether climate change is real and whether carbon and methane emissions are the cause.

Worse, there's plenty in the ranks of Republican leaders who are themselves climate deniers for the same culture war reasons their voters are. Trump's appointment to head the Environmental Protection Agency (EPA), Scott Pruitt, appears to be one of those people. Trump's choice to put Pruitt in his position also suggests that Trump views the climate change issue mainly as a way to troll liberals, and not as an actual issue that impacts real people's lives.

Pruitt rose to the top of the list for potential EPA chiefs because, during the Obama years, he led the charge to stop the Obama administration from enacting the Clean Power Plan, which was meant to drastically reduce carbon admissions from power plants. The Clean Power Plan was a signature Obama achievement, both in its aims and its methodology. The administration was widely known in policy wonk corners for seeking creative technocratic solutions to sticky problems, and the Clean Power Plan—which was designed to give states broad freedom to decide how they reduced emissions, so long as they met their goals—was a crowning example of that governing philosophy.

Pruitt, however, doesn't give two shits about the cleverness or flexibility or even the focus on local control that is supposedly precious to conservatives. He instead appears motivated by an abiding desire to keep coal power plants from shutting down. To make the whole thing even more aggravating, Pruitt's affection for coal doesn't make any sense from an economic perspective. It's hard to avoid the conclusion that one of the main reasons he and his boss Trump have such a hard-on for filthy, inefficient coal is that it's the fuel source that most upsets liberals.

To understand this, it helps to understand that coal is, even without federal pressure, dying off as a fuel source. The energy industry is moving away from it for reasons that are more economic than moral.

"Donald Trump is wrong again—it's not government regulation that's killing off the coal industry," Paul Rosenberg wrote for Salon. "It's the marketplace."

As Devashree Saha chronicled at the Brookings Institute,

"Since 2000, a series of market forces—the shale gas revolution, which has eroded coal's price advantage; cost reductions in renewable energy technology; the overall flat demand in the power sector; shifts in global demand for coal; and declining coal mine labor productivity—have all contributed to coal's decline, likely more so than government regulation."

The result is that the industry is shifting towards renewable sources like wind and solar energy, as well as natural gas, which isn't great but still emits fewer greenhouse gases than coal. Both the wind and solar energy markets have seen dramatic job growth in recent years, while the number of jobs in the coal industry is declining. As the Sierra Club has carefully chronicled, nearly half the coal power plants in the country have been shut down or scheduled for retirement since 2010.

Pruitt and Trump have a habit of insinuating that these markets shifts are the result of the Obama administration waging a "war on coal," a phrase Pruitt used at a Hazard, Kentucky, event in which he announced he would be trying to end the Clean Power Plan.

The cynicism of playing that card is off the charts. The fact of the matter is that the Clean Power Plan was never put into action. It was finalized in the waning days of the Obama administration and then subject to a bunch of holds and legal action—much of it at the behest of Pruitt himself—that delayed implementation. Pruitt, more than anyone, knows that the Obama administration couldn't have successfully waged a war on coal that never really got off the ground.

To be clear, the Clean Power Plan *was* expected to accelerate the retirement rate of coal power plants. But that's because states would conclude, on their own, that the cheapest and easiest way to meet their carbon emission goals would be to get rid of coal. From an economic standpoint, that just makes sense for states to take the easy way out and kill off an already struggling industry, to replace it with more robust industries. But it just was a process that hadn't started yet.

But all this should make it clear that the main reason to oppose this shift towards renewable energy is some irrational attachment to coal power for its own sake. If the issue is profitability for the energy sector or job creation, other forms of electricity provide that with far lower emissions and, in many cases, lower costs to the industry.

Sure, there are some industry dinosaurs who made a living off coal and don't want to change their ways, even as their profits decline. Pruitt was chronicled keeping company with many of such people. The oil industry also has some strong skin in the game of preventing a shift towards cleaner energy. But ultimately, the politics of clinging to coal, even as it makes no rational sense, goes back to these culture war issues.

Trump and Pruitt clearly cling to this myth of the coal miner as some kind of exemplar of conservative white America. The working class, dirt-under-the-fingernails image of coal miners allows soft-handed reactionaries like Trump to imagine that their race-baiting, misogynist politics are still, somehow, a way of standing up for the little guy. Trump can pretend he's just defending those hapless coal miners against the "liberal elite," when of course, all he's doing is bullying people and destroying the environment in the process. He's not even really saving any jobs—if he actually cared about working people, he'd be working on programs to get them hired in new, profitable industries.

And so they prop up the coal industry, not because it makes any economic sense, but because doing so sticks it to liberals who, for entirely pragmatic reasons, want coal to be replaced with cleaner, more efficient sources of energy.

David Roberts, an environmental journalist at Vox, deemed the problem as one of "tribal epistemology," where information "is evaluated based not on conformity to common standards of evidence or correspondence to a common understanding of the world, but on whether it supports the tribe's values and goals and is vouchsafed by tribal leaders."

But it may be an even worse problem than that, as both the coal fetish and rolling coal show: The tribalism, especially on the right, has become so ingrained that ideas are rejected simply because liberals embrace them. There really is no traditional conservative value that holds that science is inherently suspect, or that protecting the environment is bad—which is why conservative parties in most other countries have been more accepting of climate science than Republicans in the United States. The hostility to environmentalism is, all too frequently, simply a rejection of liberal values because liberals hold them.

This was evident in the way that Trump reacted to the Paris Accords, an international agreement between nearly all the countries in the world to reduce greenhouse gas emissions. Trump threw a big party in the Rose Garden to announce, with maximum reality TV-style fanfare, that the United States was pulling out of the agreement. The reasons offered weren't reasons at all. Mostly it was a grab bag of lies and paranoia that journalists at the *New York Times* and the *Washington Post* swiftly debunked.

The closest that Trump got to the truth of why he was doing this ridiculous thing was when he said, "We don't want other leaders and other countries laughing at us anymore, and they won't be."

Of course, there's no evidence whatsoever that other countries were laughing at us before, though there's plenty of evidence that they're laughing at us now that we have a hateful buffoon as president. But that paranoia, along with his repeated assertions that the Paris agreement was a bad deal, points to the culture war politics that are actually motivating Trump.

Namely, he hates Obama. *Hates* Obama, who he spent years falsely accusing of being born in another country and faking his grades to get into Ivy League schools. It doesn't take a high level degree in psychiatry to understand why Trump hates Obama. Trump, as has been thoroughly demonstrated, is racist. Knowing that a black man is smarter and better and more cosmopolitan and more interesting and probably better in bed (okay, let's face it: *definitely* better in bed) than him drives Trump bonkers. This fixation with being laughed at even likely has its roots in the fact that Obama famously mocked Trump at a White House Correspondents Dinner, making fun of Trump's obsession with Obama's birth certificate.

That's why it's so easy to believe the rumors that Trump paid prostitutes to pee on a bed in a Moscow Marriott after he heard that Obama had slept in the bed. Trump is a troll, and one with a single-minded obsession on pissing on everything good that Obama has ever done. And Obama did a fuck ton of work on the Paris Accords, just as his administration did a fuck ton of work on the Clean Power Plan.

But Trump's obsession with hating Obama works for him, because it mirrors the larger obsession on the right with hating liberals and everything liberals stand for. And, in many ways, that obsession finds its purest form in anti-environmentalism.

It's relevant here to point out that climate change denialism is a conspiracy theory. It's just as irrational as believing that the Sandy

Hook shooting was faked or that the world is secretly being run by an alien race of lizard people. The way that it's mainstreamed in Republican politics has obscured this, especially as the media has, in the past, covered the issue like it's a matter of political disagreement, rather than a major political party denying scientific facts. But it is a conspiracy theory, and it's important to keep that in mind whenever the issue crops up.

To deny climate change is real is to accuse thousands of scientists around the world—as well as political leaders, journalists, anyone who can read a science article and understand it—of collectively conspiring to pass off this supposed hoax. The alleged conspirators, who number in the millions (if not billions), are accused of doing this in some larger plot to undermine capitalism. That many of them, like Angela Merkel of Germany, are business-friendly conservatives themselves is not seen as evidence against the belief that it's an international socialist hoax.

Some conservatives try to deflect by arguing that they're not saying it's a hoax, so much as they are saying there is doubt in the scientific evidence. This, of course, is hoary nonsense. There's not any doubt. There's as much of a scientific consensus for climate change as there is for gravity. Plus, the effects are becoming rapidly visible to the layperson's eye, as temperatures rise, icecaps melt, deserts grow, hurricanes become worse, and wildfires burn out of control.

But we also know that conservatives think climate change is a conspiracy because, in 2009, right wingers exposed themselves in a made-up scandal they tried to name "Climategate." What happened was simple: a few emails from climate scientists, particularly one named Michael Mann, got leaked by hackers to the press. Conservative media tried to spin the impenetrable scientific jargon in the emails as "proof" that Mann and others were conspiring to fake the evidence for climate change. Five separate investigations were held by both international and American agencies, and found absolutely no proof whatsoever for these wild accusations.

But it didn't matter. The need to believe in this conspiracy theory outweighed any interest in listening to the facts against it. Senator James Inhofe, a Republican from Oklahoma, insisted on the American inspector general conducting an investigation into "Climategate." When the inspector general concluded there was no evidence of "inappropriately manipulated data," Inhofe basically rejected the findings of an investigation he demanded.

The irony here is that the only people manipulating data and trying to hoodwink the public are conservatives. But that's not really a conspiracy theory, because they do it out in public, where everyone can see them. If they're trying to hide, they do a piss-poor job of it.

But it hardly matters, because ultimately, it's not about the facts. It's about leaning on these tribal resentments, and the endless desires of troll nation to piss off liberals. The truth of climate change isn't really a consideration. All that matters is taking shots at the hated left.

While climate change is one of the most prominently fought over issues in the country, a smaller but definitely stranger battle, conducted mainly in the American west, shows how deep the toxin of hate-everything-liberals-love goes in American conservatism. Federal lands—which encompass everything from national parks and monuments to anything maintained by the Bureau of Land Management—have increasingly become the focus of one of the uglier culture wars to crop up in recent years.

A growing number of Republicans are starting to question whether the federal government really has a right to own and manage public lands. Even an eruption of anti-government terrorism, resulting in death, has done little to check the growth of right wing radicalism on this previously uncontroversial question of whether public lands are a thing that should exist.

Occasionally, the fight over whether the federal government has a right to own wild lands makes the national media, such as the two times the ranch-owning Bundy family of Nevada had an armed standoff with the federal government. The first time, family patriarch Cliven Bundy made headlines in 2014 by gathering an armed militia to fight government demands that he pay fees, which were already below market rates, for grazing his cattle on federally owned lands. Even though it was crystal-clear Bundy was a mean old crank with a self-serving ideology, he got a sympathetic audience in places like Fox News and with some politicians like Sen. Ted Cruz.

That sympathy lasted until Bundy pulled a James Damore and said overtly racist things to the *New York Times*, saying it was a shame that black people "never learned how to pick cotton" and that they were "better off as slaves." With that, the Fox News love dried up, but the idea he was spouting—that there was something inherently wrong about the government owning land that feckless white men would love to buy up and exploit—was just gaining ground.

The Bundys got another shot at the national media in 2016, when Cliven's sons gathered another well-armed group of militiamen and took over the Malheur National Wildlife Refuge in Oregon. This time it was to protest the government holding some other ranchers responsible for arson on government lands, but really, the entire debacle—which ended with one dead in a shootout with authorities—was about advancing further this deeply radical hatred of federal land ownership.

The choice of a wildlife refuge really underlines the culture war issues and trolling impulse driving this surge in resentment over federal land ownership. Federal lands and what to do with them have become a symbol for western right wingers to attack the hated subculture of outdoorsy liberal types who have come to flourish in places like Seattle, Boulder, and even, these days, Salt Lake City. A wildlife refuge—which is associated with the camera-toting, animal-loving tourists—was the perfect target for this anti-liberal rage.

The tourism industry is on the rise out west, driven by the gorgeous vistas and a tech industry that helps finance a culture of weekend warriors who like to rock climb, kayak, and smoke weed in their North Face gear under the stars. This shift should be welcome, especially for small towns near national parks and other federal lands that bring in business from all the tourism. Plus, the hikers and bikers tend to be supportive of protecting the landscapes that many conservatives themselves will invoke when describing their love of the west. In a more rational world, the more conservative crowd and the L.L. Bean folks could join together in their love for wide open spaces and the romance of the wild west.

But no, sadly, the urge to stick it to liberals runs too deep for that. And while there are corporate interests driving much of the push to get the government out of protecting wild lands—oil and other mining interests do spend plenty of money lobbying anti-federal lands politicians—the reality is that the burgeoning radicalism on this issue is flourishing among ordinary right wingers who don't own or even work for oil companies.

Sarah Palin understood this when she led chants of "drill, baby, drill" during the 2008 election. Palin is swift to invoke the natural beauty of Alaska when speaking of why she lives where she does. But apparently the urge to irritate liberals matters more to her than the rivers and mountains she otherwise claims to love. Those delicate environments are exactly what's threatened when you drill baby drill, not just the delicate feelings of liberals who like to go hiking.

Trump probably couldn't label 5 western states on a map, but he knows all about hating whatever it is that liberals like—which is why this once utterly fringe hatred of federal land management found a home in his administration.

Trump's one rule is that whatever Obama did is illegitimate and needs undoing, and that attitude took root in his approach to the federal lands issue, when he signed an executive order demanding that Secretary Ryan Zinke "review" 27 national monuments. Unsurprisingly, most scooped up by the order were created by Obama, and the majority of the rest were designated by Bill Clinton.

Zinke didn't strike any monument designations, as some feared he might, but he did recommend shrinking many of them or opening them up to the kind of extraction and exploitation that monument designations are supposed to protect the lands from. But even this slightly less radical measure is still extremely radical. Since 1906, when the president first got the power to make these designations, the adjustments to boundaries and uses of federal lands have been small and relatively depoliticized. But in the time of trolls, even animal habitats and hiking trails are subject to screw-the-liberals politics.

It's also an issue where one can clearly see that Trump is not an anomaly, but in fact the result of a gradual shift towards radicalism on the right that has been happening for years now. One reason that Trump was open to these attacks on national monuments is that he had been lobbied heavily by a group of Republican congressmen, especially from Utah, that have a direct ideological link to the anti-federal land radicalism driving the Bundys.

Utah congressman Rob Bishop, for instance, has introduced a bill to severely undercut the Antiquities Act, which is what gives presidents the power to create national monuments in the first place. (It was the brainchild of Teddy Roosevelt, a man Republicans all swear to love even as they attack his legacy.) It would limit the area a president can designate to 640 acres, which would prevent the creation of iconic national monuments like Grand Staircase-Escalante in Utah, a preserved area that covers nearly 1.9 million acres. Bishop has also tried to pass bills that would transfer ownership of federal lands to states, where they will almost invariably be sold off to private interests.

Bishop is a kook ranting in a corner, but instead of quietly sidelining him like you might expect a rational national party to do, the Republicans who control the house made him the chairman of the House Committee on Natural Resources. That's what happens when trolling becomes your governing philosophy: A leadership role that should be reserved for someone who cares about preserving natural beauty and our country's heritage is handed to someone who wants to slice it up and sell it to the lowest bidder.

Right wing America's first loyalty is to trolling liberals. Love of the land they live on, and the planet itself, come as a distant second.

Case Study: Sam Clovis

The story of how the Trump administration does business might be best illustrated by one of the more obscure appointments made—and abandoned—in 2017, that of a right wing political operative named Sam Clovis to be the chief scientist at the U.S. Department of Agriculture (USDA).

Trump appeared to be trolling liberals with many of his appointments, but with Clovis, he outdid himself. Clovis was so singularly unqualified for his job that it was hard to imagine that his appointment served any other purpose but to infuriate liberals, by making mockery of the belief that people should have some qualifications for jobs other than being white male mediocrities who know how to kiss Trump's ass in just the way he likes it.

But it's one case that, unlike most in this sad book, had a somewhat happy ending. Clovis was done in by the very corruption that most in the Trump administration manage to get away with, despite the mountains of very public evidence against them.

It's no secret that the Trump campaign was unable to attract talented people, even by the artificially lowered Republican standards. Instead, the campaign was staffed by a bunch of has-beens and nobodies who correctly grasped that their only chance to get any real power in the world was putting all their money on a long shot bet on Trump. Clovis was one of these people. After retiring from the Air Force, Clovis settled in Iowa, a place where a man could rise high as a Republican power player, despite being gifted with very few political talents.

Clovis ran for office in Iowa and lost a couple of times, but mostly he made his name by being a local talk show radio host, while making some money on the side by teaching business classes at a community college. But Iowa is the first state in both parties' primary contests, and a caucus state to boot, so Clovis managed to gain some grudging respect in Republican power circles, because he was able to wield his big fish in a small pond power to help secure caucus wins for otherwise unviable candidates like Rick Santorum in 2012. But he couldn't rise higher than being an Iowa caucus player. That is until the Trump campaign, desperate for any warm bodies, picked him up as a policy advisor.

No big surprise, but Clovis is a barking loon. He denies climate change is real, calling it "junk science." He's a bigot through and through, one who implied that Barack Obama was born in Kenya and called Obama's black attorney general, Eric Holder, a "racist black." He is also wildly homophobic, claiming that "LGBT behavior" is an "aberration" and sexual orientation is a choice.

The Trump administration is stuffed full of science-hating bigots, of course, but Clovis's nomination was especially egregious, since, by law, the chief scientist at the USDA must be from "among distinguished scientists with specialized training or significant experience in agricultural research, education or economics." Clovis's doctorate in public administration clearly didn't meet the requirements, but in Trump's America, being a white guy counts for more than considerations like actually knowing how to do the job you're hired to do.

Clovis's lack of qualifications were especially troubling in light of the very serious nature of the job he was supposed to do. The chief scientist at the USDA handles around $3 billion in research grants, which are meant to fund work helping American farmers develop best practices to feed our country and compete on international agricultural markets.

Scientific research in agriculture is more important than ever, as global warming is rapidly changing the environment farmers have to work in. Water is drying up in some places and in other places, it's raining more than ever. Temperatures are shifting away from the optimal ones plants were bred to grow in. Countries like Canada and Russia might start being able to grow in places that were previously too cold for agriculture. Without scientific research to deal with these problems, American farmers could be very screwed, and American consumers could see food prices soar. By appointing Clovis, someone who flatly denies that any of this is even happening, Trump issued a fuck-you to both people who grow and eat food in the United States.

Why Trump did this is a bit mysterious, though most political watchers assume that it's just straight cronyism. Clovis was one of the few Republican operators willing to throw in with the Trump campaign in the early days, and the administration likely wanted to pay him back by giving him a salary and an office. The USDA chief scientist seemed like an easy throwaway job to give this guy, and they could sort of justify it by pointing out that Clovis was from Iowa, as if everyone there is an expert in agriculture. It's very much like the Trump administration to neither know nor care that it's actually a very important job that, if done wrong, could drastically harm the quality of life for everyday Americans. Or that the appointment was likely illegal, because Clovis didn't meet the qualifications outlined by law.

But as the day of Clovis's confirmation hearing neared, he was derailed from his path towards being a well-paid incompetent crony ruining an important federal office. The issue was, of all things, Russia.

Special counsel Robert Mueller—assigned to investigate and prosecute any possible crimes stemming from the Trump campaign's many, many troubling links to the same Russian government and oligarchs believed to be behind illegal U.S. election meddling—announced his investigation's first guilty plea in October 2017. A Trump campaign foreign policy advisor named George Papadopoulos lied to the FBI about his dealings with Russian agents, apparently because he believed that's what the Trump administration wanted from him. Shortly thereafter, it was revealed that one of the people on the campaign that Papadopoulos was reporting on his Russian activities to was Clovis. Yep, the USDA guy.

After Papadopoulos's guilty plea was made public, Clovis gave up any hope of sitting in an office getting paid to ruin the lives of scientists working to keep your food affordable and healthy. Shortly before his scheduled confirmation, Clovis withdrew his nomination. Instead, he went to testify, still in secret at time of writing, to a grand jury about court documents indicating he eagerly encouraged Papadopoulos to set up secretive meetings overseas with Russian operatives. Emails showed that Clovis was aware of meetings Papadopoulos had with a professor, clearly operating as a Russian cut-out, who had offered Papadopoulos "dirt" on Hillary Clinton in the form of stolen emails.

While Clovis's PR people ran around minimizing Clovis's interest in Russia, a *USA Today* reporter named Steve Reilly dug up a YouTube campaign video from Clovis's failed 2014 Senate run in which Clovis defended Russia in their efforts to annex the Crimean Peninsula—which happened a day after Clovis posted the video.

"You must remember that Russia, the nation that we know, the historical Russia, actually originated in Ukraine," Clovis argued in his video. "This is important for us to remember because Russians will want to expand back again into those old boundaries, the old empire."

The choice to record this video was an odd one for a senatorial candidate from Iowa. Not that national politicians shouldn't have opinions on foreign policy issues, but most Iowa voters, it's safe to say, aren't really that interested in the legality of Russia's efforts to dissolve Ukrainian independence. Clovis just didn't have an opinion about this matter, but was really eager to talk about it, going on Radio Iowa to talk up his views on Ukrainian-Russian relations for voters who were probably unaware of and unconcerned about the conflict in the first place. The rush forward to find any microphone he could speak into on this issue was just straight up weird.

It's possible that nothing sinister or conspiratorial is going on. It might just be that the Trump campaign was chock-a-block full of Russia enthusiasts who were, due to their fan boy-ish love of Putin's authoritarian regime, laughably easy for Russian operators to manipulate. As the Clovis video shows, even before Trump's weird Russia-loving campaign surged into prominence, troll nation was starting to feel the first stirrings of love for Putin, who they saw as a right wing dreamboat, a manly man compared to Obama.

"People are looking at Putin as one who wrestles bears and drills for oil," Sarah Palin gushed in 2014. "They look at our president as one who wears mom jeans and equivocates and bloviates."

Victor Davis Hanson of the *National Review*, while reluctantly agreeing that journalist-murdering and jailing political opponents is bad, waxed poetically about how Putin is "an unpredictable, unapologetic brute force of nature" who just takes what he wants, compared to the alleged pansies of "the West" who "continually overthink, hyperagonize, and nuance to death every idea, every issue, and every thought in terror that it might not be 100 percent fair, completely unbiased, absolutely justified."

"IT LOOKS LIKE OBAMA IS PUTIN'S BITCH," crowed the right wing bloggers at *Astute Bloggers*, showcasing what this argument looks like when stripped of pseudo-intellectual justifications.

It's troll logic boiled down to its essence. Most of these conservatives would admit, however begrudgingly, that Putin is a bad guy and that things like functionally banning open homosexuality or free speech are bad things to do. However, Putin and Obama didn't get along, conservatives hate Obama, and so many on the right started getting Putin-curious. The nationalistic bent of much authoritarian Russian rhetoric—such as nationalistic claims over the Ukraine—clearly grabbed the imagination of people like Clovis, as well.

There are many characters in Trump's circle that are strange, unqualified, corrupt, or bigoted—and are usually some combination of all four of these things. But for my money, the story of Sam Clovis might be the best example of what happens when you decide to run a campaign and then a presidential administration based on little more than the whims of right wing assholes ranting in the comments section.

Clovis is an incompetent clown who appears to have selected most of his opinions based on the metric of liberals-will-hate-this. Worse, he got a bad case of Putin googly-eyes that may have helped him open the door to Russian collusion with the Trump campaign. That's the depths of depravity that knee-jerk anti-liberalism can send a modern conservative to: Playing footsie with a murderous authoritarian who hates democracy, all because hey, at least he pisses off the liberals.

Chapter 5

Health Care

Sometimes in the past year, I would find myself wondering if Republicans ever regret the day they decided to grant the Affordable Care Act the nickname "Obamacare."

In 2009, it probably seemed like a smashing idea. Barack Obama was new to the office, but Republicans were already quite aware that his name alone triggered a whole mess of inchoate rage in the conservative base, a frothing-at-the-mouth fury that a black man with a name like that would dare sit in the White House.

"Obamacare" wasn't even the only word that obtained the prefix "Obama." At the same time as the debate for the ACA warmed up, the right wing urban legend networks were aflame with stories about "Obamaphones," mythical free cell phones one received from the government simply by being on welfare. In some versions of the tale, a person had to be black to get their hands on the free phones. As early as October 2009—five months before Obama signed the ACA into law—FactCheck.org was debunking the myth of the "Obamaphone."

Attaching Obama's name to anything likely seemed like a genius way to get the base so whipped up in outrage at the health care bill that there was no way they would notice that the actual provisions of the bill would actually help them and their families obtain afford-able health care. As the "Obamaphone" example shows, it's clear that many right wingers were ready to attach all sorts of other insinu-ations to the use of "Obama" as an adjective: that it must be some sort of program for lazy, dark-skinned welfare cheats, an image that seems to be a permanent fixture in the conservative imagination.

Betting that right wingers were more interested in culture war than the intricacies of health care policy worked out for Republi-cans. As Democrats fanned out across the country to hold town halls to explain the health care bill, they got rushed by crowds of irate white people who were painfully ignorant about this bill they hated. Attempts to patiently explain the realities of the bill failed. The town hall crowds, who quickly formed into a move-ment nicknamed the "Tea Party," only knew that Democrats wanted this bill—and so Tea Partiers hated it.

While Republican efforts to demonize the legislation failed to stop it from passing, it's arguable that the controversy gave con-servative forces leverage to remove some of the more progressive provisions from the bill. The public option—which would have created some market competition for private insurance compa-nies and made sure that even people living in remote areas had at least one insurance option on the federal exchanges—was the most notable provision Democrats had to give up during debate.

But while there was some short term political gain for

Republicans, they had underestimated how much the conservative base is motivated by this nihilistic urge to destroy anything perceived as "liberal" or "Democrat." That antagonism doubles whenever racial and gendered prejudices are aroused. The ACA had both in spades, both in the way that the bill was associated with the first black president and in the way that it helped secure contraception access, which the conservative press treated like some kind of giveaway program for sluts.

Republicans gleefully kept stoking the resentments of troll nation by repeatedly making a pointless show of efforts to "repeal" the ACA. Between 2011, when Republicans gained control of the House of Representatives, and 2014, Republicans passed 54 bills to either repeal or drastically rewrite the ACA in a way that would likely kill it. These efforts were pure theater, typically ignored by a Senate that knew Obama would veto any such bills anyway.

Meanwhile, the provisions of the ACA started coming into effect and were largely popular with the public—even Republican voters. When Pew Research Center polled voters in 2016, they found that healthy majorities of Republicans liked every major provision of the bill, except the fines for not having health insurance (which they likely did not understand are necessary to keep premiums from spiraling out of control).

Letting your kid stay on your insurance plan until 26?—86 percent of Republicans were for it. Mandating co-pay free coverage of preventive services?—77 percent of Republicans supported it. Seventy-two percent approved of the creation of the health care exchanges. Over two-thirds approved of expanding Medicaid and giving low income people help to pay for health care. Sixty-three percent approved of the provision barring insurance companies from denying coverage based on pre-existing conditions.

Republican voters, it turns out, like the Affordable Care Act. What they hate is Obamacare. The problem for Republican leaders is that both are the same law. You can't get rid of Obamacare without destroying the Affordable Care Act.

There are many thousands of complex explanations for why Republicans, once they finally captured the presidency and both houses of Congress, found themselves unable to pass a bill to "repeal and replace Obamacare," despite promising to do so for the better part of a decade. There's a lot of truth in many of those complicated explanations, but ultimately it came down to this: they had no idea how to repeal "Obamacare" while leaving the Affordable Care Act in its place.

Not that any reader should feel an ounce of pity for Senate Majority Leader Mitch McConnell or Speaker of the House Paul Ryan, and not just because both are vile men who would take away millions of people's health care in a heartbeat, if they could just get the votes. Their inability to move repeal-and-replace bills—they tried and failed twice in the spring and summer of 2017—is their just desserts for relying on culture war politics to drum up political hostility towards concepts, like universal health care, that should be no more controversial than universal highway systems or universal public education.

(Both of which Republicans are trying to make more controversial, but find it's hard, because there's fewer scare stories about greedy sluts and welfare cheats to attach to the concept of public schools or open highways.)

The impulses that have created troll nation—resentment, bigotry, nihilism—are extremely powerful political forces. But they are their own kind of Frankenstein's monster. Now that millions of Americans have organized their political identities and ideologies around the concept of sticking-it-to-liberals, they cannot be reasoned with or corralled. That's why troll nation elevated Trump in the first place, because no one else in politics so embodies that mindless urge to bully, coupled with a complete indifference to the realities of governance.

Trump's position as King Troll and his single-minded obsession with laying waste to Obama's legacy, made what happened next entirely predictable: If Republicans weren't going to get rid of Obamacare, then he would do whatever he could to destroy it, consequences be damned.

Trump is a man whose first thought every day upon waking up and going to bed is how much he can't stand Obama. The suffering of millions doesn't even rate, in Trump's mind, compared to his desire to dominate a man whose charisma, good looks, and easy intelligence makes Trump burn with an unquenchable fear of inadequacy.

So Trump set about trying to break Obamacare. His administration deliberately failed to advertise the sign-up period, driving down enrollment numbers. They planned huge amounts of maintenance for exchange websites during peak sign-up hours, frustrating users into giving up. Then, in a stroke to really screw things up, Trump signed an executive order designed to jack up premiums, particularly on middle class families who don't qualify for discounts or subsidies under the ACA.

The way this works is wonky and boring, but the quick-and-dirty version is this: Trump's executive order declared an end to subsidy payments to insurance companies that offset low income discounts. He also ordered tweaks to funnel young, healthy consumers out of the mainstream insurance market, which would drive up costs for the sicker, older people who have to have comprehensive plans.

As usual, there's an elaborate pundit explanation for why Trump did this, and then there's the more realistic explanation that takes into account Trump's utter inability to understand anything more complex than a picture book. The elaborate pundit explanation is that Trump was threatening to tank the ACA as a negotiating tactic: by jacking up rates on consumers, he was hoping to cause enough panic in Congress that Democrats would vote for any bill the Republicans offered to replace the ACA, just to stop the bleeding. This theory, however, depends on the implausible notion that Trump has the attention span to craft anything resembling "strategy."

The likelier explanation is that Trump is a nihilistic vandal who is too stupid to actually understand what "Obamacare" is. This is a man who told the *New York Times*, "[Y]ou're 21 years old, you start working and you're paying $12 a year for insurance, and by the time you're 70, you get a nice plan." He isn't someone who knows what health insurance is, making him entirely incapable of dealing with policy negotiations around it.

Trump, like the Tea Party morons who flooded town halls to scream about "death panels" in 2009, has no real idea what's in the law or how it works. All he wants is to destroy Obama. If Trump could pay prostitutes to pee all over Obamacare, he would. Since that's not possible, he'll have to settle for ruining the American health care system for no logical reason. So his team came up with a bunch of policies to raise premiums and, sensing an opportunity to destroy something liberals like, he went for it.

Trump's language during the announcement of the executive order exposed the obsessed, personal nature of his vendetta.

"Obamacare is finished. It's dead. It's gone. You shouldn't

even mention it," he raved. "It's gone. There is no such thing as Obamacare anymore."

As Josh Marshall at Talking Points Memo noted, it was a "febrile set of demands about Obamacare that recall movie mobster dialog" and Trump's tone was "more hot and out of control than I've seen so far, even from Trump."

We can all safely assume that what unhinged Trump is not the knowledge that some 35-year-old Wal-Mart manager gets to see a doctor this year. It's about Obama and Trump's deeply racist urge to wipe all evidence off the map that Obama ever mattered.

To be entirely fair, Trump did seem to enjoy hearing pundits speculate that his ruining the ACA was some kind of negotiating tactic. He does enjoy hearing that he makes "deals," even though his one strategy—bellowing threats that he often forgets about moments later—is the sort of thing real negotiators roll out on the Do Not Do list at deal-making school.

But while Trump doesn't know much about anything, one thing he grasps, intuitively at least, is the psychology of troll nation. After all, he's a pure specimen of the resentment and rage that defines them. His communications to the public about this decision suggested that he was confident that he could wreck the health care system, blame the Democrats, and get away with it with his supporters.

"Any increase in ObamaCare premiums is the fault of the Democrats for giving us a 'product' that never had a chance of working," he tweeted, which is a lie, because his own policy was designed to raise premiums.

This is the bet Trump is making: that the average Republican voter's irrational hatred of Democrats is so all-consuming, they would happily pay 20 percent more a year in health care costs in order to maintain their loathing.

It's a bet that goes against most political wisdom. The typical political wisdom is that whatever party holds the White House gets blamed for everything that goes wrong, even in cases where it's completely out of the president's control. For instance, Obama got blamed by voters for a lot of gridlock and inability to fix serious problems like income inequality, even though those problems were the fault of a Republican-controlled Congress that desired both gridlock and income inequality. It's arguable that this tendency to blame the president's party for *everything* is why Hillary Clinton lost some of Obama's voters in 2016. What's completely inarguable is that the reason Mitch McConnell deliberately created gridlock was that he believed that voters would blame Obama and Obama only for it.

Trump is making a different bet, which is that no matter how much he deliberately fucks with the country, his voters will happily lap up whatever lie he feeds them about who else's fault it is. He hasn't really even hidden this belief, bragging during the campaign that he could "shoot somebody and wouldn't lose voters."

How well his gambit works remains to be seen. I think Trump is partially right and partially wrong. Where he's right is in his understanding of his own avid supporters, the members of troll nation. He's probably right to bet these folks would live in a trash pile as long as they believe they can force liberals to live in a shit pile. Trump sees his followers as suckers whose resentments can be used to get them to swallow all sorts of indignities, and so far, there's no evidence to contradict him.

Where he's likely wrong is in believing this to be true of the country as a whole. Troll nation's power is, and this cannot be emphasized enough, a direct result of serious flaws in our electoral system that render it undemocratic. Trump lost the popular vote by nearly 3 million votes, and was only saved by an electoral college system that gives more weight to rural and suburban votes than to urban votes. Even then, his victory was sliver thin, so much so that if the election had been held a week before or a week after, it's likely he would have lost the election.

In this way, Trump conducts himself more like a cult leader than a politician. Instead of trying to build a coalition of voters, he focuses most of his attention on feeding the cultural resentments of troll nation. That works well to increase their fervor and devotion to him, because they really do care more about hating black football players kneeling during the national anthem than they care about health care premiums. But there is some percentage of people, however small, who voted for Trump in 2016 who simply didn't realize that his reckless persona wasn't just a clown act, but is in fact his actual personality—and that he really will take away your health care if he thinks doing so will somehow hurt Obama.

Not, to be clear, that this means 2020 is in the bag for Democrats. As 2016 demonstrated, the world is a chaotic place and anything can happen, and it's unwise to bet that the United States will be able to get its act together to prevent something as seemingly easy to prevent as electing Donald Trump as president.

Still, the whole health care debacle really lays out, in crystal clear terms, the political realities of troll nation: even though wrecking the health care system is a really bad idea, and even though Republican voters like the provisions of the ACA, the logic of sticking it to the liberals is still the guiding principle of the right—and especially of Donald Trump. Trump's not wrong to believe that he could take away their health care, and most Republicans will still vote for him. That's how the tribal politics of the 21st century right wing work. It's so all-consuming that, as long as troll nation has power, the ACA is never really safe.

Case Study: Steve Bannon

Steve Bannon, the former head of Breitbart who had the official title of Donald Trump's chief strategist for a few short months, is probably the greatest evidence we have that Trumpism is the first post-modern fascist movement. Authoritarian, proto-fascist and outright fascist movements of the past seem, to this non-historian at least, to proceed without much sense of self-awareness. Bannon's approach, however, is a sort of meta-fascism. One always gets the sense, watching him, that he is watching himself perform the role of fascist demagogue, and calculatingly models his rhetoric and approach on the greatest hits of fascism's past.

To be clear, fascists of years past always had a sense of theater. The KKK gave themselves elaborate titles like Grand Dragon and wore costumes with elaborate insignia. The Nazis perfected the art of the operatic political rally. Augusto Pinochet, like many other dictators in history, probably even showered while wearing medals and sashes and listening to dramatic, patriotic music.

But these folks mostly came on their near-campy fixation with high drama naturally. With Bannon, there's always this lingering sense that he decided that he was going to be the man who revived 20th century fascism, and so is consciously modeling his rhetoric (though not his clothes—the man in a grotesque slob) after authoritarians who have come before.

Bannon is to the KKK as Netflix's *Stranger Things* is to Steven Spielberg's oeuvre. It's fascism as a retro fad.

Which doesn't mean he's insincere, to be clear. All one needs to do is watch a video of Bannon speaking for more than 60 seconds at a clip to grasp that the man is an entirely sincere maniac. That he's playing a role doesn't mean he's playing around. It's just that he has a nostalgic quality to his hate-mongering and populist posturing that is hard to miss, and not a little peculiar. Of all the things from the past to get obsessively sentimental about, it's just straight up odd to fixate on fascist movements, especially since all that history shows things rarely work out well for those who get really into the idea of turning modern democracies into authoritarian ethno-states.

Then again, there's always some guy who thinks he can succeed where others have failed. Hitler may have ended up dead and with his body thrown in a river, our modern fascists seem to be thinking, but that's because he was bad at Twitter.

Bannon likes to pose as a dirt-under-the-nails man of the people, but like most of the self-assigned leaders of right wing populism, he's far more of an elitist than those liberals he decries. Bannon got his start, with a Harvard MBA, as an investment banker at Goldman Sachs during the absolute height of the yuppie era, the '80s. He then went on to join another community he now likes to stigmatize as too cosmopolitan—Hollywood, as a film and TV producer. It was there that he got into right wing conspiracy theories, eventually joining forces with Andrew Breitbart, a right wing provocateur who ran a site called Big Government that eventually morphed into Breitbart News.

Breitbart liked to portray himself as a muckraking journalist, but in reality, he is better understood as a racist propagandist. His favorite strategy was targeting people or organizations associated with the fight for racial equality and peddling fake stories to discredit them—and ideally, getting those fake stories into the mainstream media.

Breitbart launched his site with a fake "exposé" of ACORN, a non-profit organization that helped low income people with voting registration and housing. In a series of misleadingly edited videos, Breitbart and his accomplices, James O'Keefe and Hannah Giles, falsely accused the organization of aiding and abetting sex trafficking. Even though the accusations were unfounded and frankly ridiculous, the group's government funding was stripped. Eventually, ACORN simply collapsed.

Breitbart played a similar dirty trick on the Georgia state director of rural development, a black woman named Shirley Sherrod. A video of her denouncing racism against all people, white and black, was deceptively edited to make it sound like she hated white people. She, too, was fired—and later, like ACORN, exonerated.

That's the kind of racist scum Andrew Breitbart was, until he died in 2012. At this point, Bannon, who was on the board of Breitbart News, took over and the site was renamed, simply, "Breitbart."

More than any other single organization, Breitbart is the core of troll nation. As when Andrew Breitbart was alive, there is no misinformation so false, no racism so over-the-top, that it can't be justified as publishable because it aggravates the liberals. The site literally has a tag called "black crime," devoted to portraying black people as criminals and delighting readers who just know that kind of in-your-face racism really makes those "libtards" cry.

To be clear, the misogyny and racism of Breitbart's editors and readers is entirely sincere. However, it's also clear that their business model is built around the belief that right wing readers click headlines based on what they think will anger the liberals the most. Unlike most 20th century right wing publications, which at least tried to maintain the myth that they were being written by reasonable people who are making sincere arguments, Breitbart headlines are deliberately provocative. The fun for readers is in wallowing in the mud and thumbing your nose at anyone who thinks you're dirty.

"Bill Kristol: Republican Spoiler, Renegade Jew," blared a recent example.

"Does Feminism Make Women Ugly?" read another. (Just guess what the conclusion is!)

"The Confederate Flag Proclaims A Glorious Heritage," reads another. (This was published less than two weeks after Confederate flag-loving Dylann Roof murdered 9 people in a church for the simple reason that they were black.)

"NBC Covers Up Evidence of Immigrant Crime Wave," proclaimed a 2015 headline.

A recent quiz, published in *Slate*, demonstrated that many Breitbart headlines—about immigration, crime, nationalism—were direct echoes of headlines published in KKK papers in the 1920s. Readers trying to differentiate between Breitbart headlines and KKK newsletter stories were right about 62 percent of the time, only about 12 percentage points better than one would get with a coin flip.

Bannon leveraged his position at Breitbart into a role in the Trump campaign and then, finally, into a position as a chief strategist at the White House. After a few months, however, he was let go, no doubt because his obnoxious personality was drawing bad press. And, perhaps more importantly, he was threatening Trump's position as the biggest asshole in the White House, and Trump is notoriously insecure and unwilling to let anyone be better than him at anything. But while Bannon's not drawing a federal paycheck anymore, he still reportedly speaks on the phone with Trump on the regular—doing the same job, but without having to get out of bed and put a suit on, which no doubt is more to his liking anyway.

Bannon speaks in a pseudo-intellectual dialect that is meant to paint his sewer-dwelling racist views in a grandiose and impressive light. He peppers his rants with historical and literary allusions that he clearly is hoping that his audience doesn't understand well enough to recognize as bullshit. In an interview he gave Charlie Rose after he was let go from the White House, Bannon gave a typical performance of covering for his incoherence by rattling off a bunch of historical references:

> Look at the 19th century. What built America's called the American system, from Hamilton to Polk to Henry Clay to Lincoln to the Roosevelts. A system of protection of our manufacturing, financial system that lends to manufacturers, OK, and the control of our borders. Economic nationalism is what this country was built on.

It sounds very learned and erudite, with all those names, right? But, as Jamelle Bouie at *Slate* pointed out, there's not really a clear throughline between those names and, more importantly, it erases the fact that enslaved people and immigrants did the actual work of building the infrastructure Bannon is praising.

But Bannon's favorite allusion to make himself sound smart is a 1973 novel called *The Camp of Saints*, written by a loony French racist named Jean Raspail. Name-dropping an obscure French novel is très pretentious, but even though it's written in French, the book is a piece of trash and is very, very, very racist. Raspail literally portrays dark-skinned immigrants as people who eat shit and who are eager to "invade" white, Western nations to turn them into supposed savages.

"Indians stream on shore, trampling to death the left-wing

radicals who came to welcome them," Paul Blumenthal and JM Rieger of HuffPost write, explaining the plot.

The book describes black and brown people as "thousands of wretched creatures" who are "starting to rot, all wormy inside." Raspail imagines a shipful of Indians as a writhing orgy, writing, "Everywhere, rivers of sperm" then he imagines "streaming over bodies, oozing between breasts, and buttocks, and thighs, and lips, and fingers."

At the time of publication, the book sold well, because terrible people are always with us. But reviewers from the period were less impressed. Paul Gray, reviewing the English translation in *Time* in 1975, said it was a book for those "who have always wondered what it would feel like to be worked over by the Gestapo."

"The publishers are presenting *The Camp of the Saints* as a major event," the contemporaneous *Kirkus Review* noted, "and it probably is, in much the same sense that *Mein Kampf* was a major event."

Bannon fucking *loves* this book. HuffPost found four instances of Bannon referencing it over a period of less than two years. In every reference, he treats the book like great literature and a reasonable prediction of what will happen if Europe and the United States continue to allow immigration.

"It's been almost a *Camp of the Saints*-type invasion into Central and then Western and Northern Europe," he said, in a typical example.

Bannon is a monster, but, as with Trump, monsters are hot with the Republican base these days. After all, if you really want to scandalize those snowflake liberals, well, calling people of color turd-eating animals is a pretty swift way to get the job done.

The funny thing about trolls, though, is that once they get the taste for trolling, their appetites grow and grow. They become restless trolling the usual targets and start wanting to expand their trolling horizons. Pissing off liberals with overt racism stops feeling like a challenge. The troll wishes for something more, something to really test his trolling powers.

So it was with Bannon. After years of trolling the left with race-baiting and making up fake scandals about Democratic politicians and liberal institutions, I think he got bored. Liberals, with all their morals and do-gooding, are just way too easy to ruffle. So he set his sights on Republicans, and set himself a new goal: could he, through the power of trolling, literally take over an entire political party?

Bannon has publicly set this as his exciting new goal, now that he, through the Trump win, has accumulated political capital. "Right now, it's a season of war against a GOP establishment," he thundered during a 2017 speech at a Values Voter summit.

But, as Greg Sargent of the *Washington Post* wrote, Bannon's war "isn't really a battle over policy or ideology"—both the Bannonites and the establishment want to cut taxes for the rich and destroy the American health care system—but really a fight over aesthetics.

The Bannon wing wants the white identity politics and *Camp of Saints*-style racism up front and center. The traditional Republican party prefers the old style of insinuating racism without ever coming right out and saying it. It's really come down to a war between the obnoxious trolls and those who prefer a note of gentility while they destroy your grandmother's Social Security benefits.

Team Bannon appears to be winning this war, even as the man himself is out of the White House. Not only do they have a man in the Oval Office who seems to think his main job is harassing

NFL players on Twitter, but the Bannonites are running off the handful of Republicans who want more dignified proceedings as they strip away human rights and give all your money to the rich.

In the fall of 2017, both Sen. Jeff Flake of Arizona and Sen. Bob Corker of Tennessee threw in the towel, announcing their retirements from the once-noble congressional body. Both are far-right ideologues that voted for Trump's agenda the vast majority of the time, so their decisions weren't really about policy. As Flake explained in his speech about his ending his Senate career, it's about "the reckless provocations, most often for the pettiest and most personal reasons" coming from the White House. So, nothing really substantive—he just prefers not having a sadistic white guy in charge tweet invective during his morning bowel movement.

Ultimately, Bannon's war on the GOP is just Gamergate, but applied to stuffed-shirt Republicans, instead of women in the video game industry. The strategy is the same: Troll and pester until the targets give up, and then the trolls can claim victory. It's not just politics of personal destruction, but politics for no other purpose than personal destruction. Sadly, Bannon's power and popularity is no fluke, but just another piece of evidence that this is what defines the American right in the post-Obama era.

Chapter 6

Guns

During the 2008 campaign, the conservative media, desperate to create a faux controversy to hang around Barack Obama's neck, seized on a comment he made about rural working class white voters, that they "get bitter, they cling to guns or religion or antipathy to people who aren't like them or anti-immigrant sentiment."

The faux outrage at Obama's supposed elitism became one of the stations of the right wing cross. Even though he's been out of office over a year, conservative pundits still drag the comment out on a regular basis for some ritualistic outrage.

As usually is true of these things, the comment in context is not at all what the conservative press made it out to be. Obama wasn't trying to demonize rural white working class voters. He was trying to make them more sympathetic to wealthy liberals in San Francisco who were at a Democratic fundraiser. The fuller comments make this clear:

You go into some of these small towns in Pennsylvania, and like a lot of small towns in the Midwest, the jobs have been gone now for 25 years and nothing's replaced them. And they fell through the Clinton Administration, and the Bush Administration, and each successive administration has said that somehow these communities are gonna regenerate and they have not. And it's not surprising then they get bitter, they cling to guns or religion or antipathy to people who aren't like them or anti-immigrant sentiment or anti-trade sentiment as a way to explain their frustrations.

(To be fair, Hillary Clinton, who was locked in a vicious primary with him, also exploited the remark by taking it out of context. Karma came to get her, though, as her similar 2016 comments, where she distinguished the "basket of deplorables" that support Trump from his supporters "who feel that the government has let them down, the economy has let them down, nobody cares about them, nobody worries about what happens to their lives and their futures, and they're just desperate for change." She got a similarly unfair treatment in the press by those who pretended not to notice the context.)

The abuse Obama got is doubly ironic as, 8 years later, his theory that Republican voters turn to racism because of their economic insecurity has been embraced by many in both the mainstream media and in the conservative media, mostly because they want to have a better explanation for Trump's ascendancy, and for the existence of troll nation generally, than simply assuming a lot of Americans are just racist fucking shitbirds. Calling conservative voters "bitter clingers" is, at this late date, considered a compliment, since the alternative—that the 46.4 percent of the country that voted for Trump would rather put a racist in office than a woman—is just more than some folks can really handle.

Considering that the median Trump voter made $11,000 more a year than the average Clinton voter—and really, that undersells it, when you consider that Clinton voters tend to live in cities with higher costs of living than suburban Trump voters enjoy—I tend to attribute the bitterness and bigotry that drove troll nation to elect Trump to office to something other than economic insecurity. But I do agree with Obama's famous comments on two points: 21st century right wingers are bitter and they do cling to guns.

Nowadays, most political pundits have come around to understanding that guns are not actually a "rights" issue, but a culture war issue. Like oversized trucks and protesting at abortion clinics, guns have no practical value, but are just something that conservatives wield to assert their identity and, of course, irritate liberals. Well, there's also some masculine overcompensation going on there, too, but unfortunately, no one has done an in-depth study comparing penis size to arsenal size, so that will have to be left to the realm of speculation.

I grew up in rural Texas and around guns, and I can safely say that most of them are useless for most people. Even hunting isn't as popular a hobby anymore, and many of the guns that the industry is pushing hardest to sell—handguns, assault rifles—are not really meant for killing quail or even deer. Most gun owners use them to feel tough and manly and dominant. Unfortunately, that just increases the odds they'll reach for a gun when they're arguing with someone or otherwise feeling insecure. Sure, guns are fun to shoot, but with all the death and destruction, they're just not worth the hassle.

For self-defense, guns are worse than useless. If you own a gun, you're many more times likely to be shot by that gun than you are to use it in self-defense. One study in Philadelphia showed that carrying a gun means you are 4.5 times more likely to be shot during an assault than someone who isn't carrying a gun. For every instance in which a gun is used successfully in self-defense in the U.S., there are 7 assaults or murders, 11 suicide attempts, and 4 accidents in the home—all involving a gun.

Owning a gun is dumb for the vast majority of people, and this fact is starting to sink into minds nationwide. The percentage of Americans who own guns has been on a relatively steady decline for decades. In 1978, a little over half of Americans had a gun in the house. Now it's down to 36 percent.

This is good for those Americans who enjoy not getting shot, but for the gun industry, the shrinking customer base is a cause for worry. So they've landed on a solution that has been profitable for them and horrific for the rest of us: convince the people who do buy guns to buy a whole lot more of them.

The gun industry has two things going for it. One, gun owners are a gullible group. Two, they have successfully disguised the industry's marketing arm as a politically oriented non-profit: the National Rifle Association, known as the NRA.

The NRA started off as a rifle club, back in the days when hunting and sport shooting were more popular, but nowadays its two main functions are to scare politicians away from any reasonable gun safety legislation and—and this is probably more important—to convince conservatives to spend their kid's college education fund on guns. The best part is that the NRA accepts donations from ordinary Americans to market guns to them. It's hard to find another industry that has convinced its customers to pay them directly for the advertising.

In recent years, the NRA has finely honed its pitch to the gun-buying audience: liberals are bad and the best way to aggravate liberals is to buy more guns.

Half the time, NRA ads and videos, which are well-funded and shared widely online, don't even bother to pretend to have any other message about sporting or safety. For instance, as I was writing this, the top video on the NRA TV webpage was a minute-long video, which doesn't even mention guns, which is strictly about denying that CNN is a legitimate news organization. It's a claim bolstered by a weird conspiracy theory about the network "colluding" with Hillary Clinton.

(In reality, CNN really led the way on giving Trump an unheard-of amount of campaign coverage, which helped pave the way to Trump's victory. It wasn't *collusion*, to be clear. Most media experts believe the choice to air every dumb Trump fart and utterance was due to CNN's head, Jeff Zucker, believing Trump was good for ratings. But it was a choice that fucked over the country.)

Any random day on NRA TV, the organization's main propaganda arm, most of the featured content is centered around the message that a nefarious liberal elite is taking over your country and that the true patriot obsesses over and hates these people.

One example, from NRA spokeswoman Dana Loesch, was a video that went viral in June 2016. In it, she framed conservative America as the hostage of a liberal elite that is seemingly all-powerful—though still somehow not powerful enough to win an election, even with the majority of the popular vote.

They use their media to assassinate real news. They use their schools to teach children that their president is another

Hitler. They use their movie stars and singers and award shows to repeat their narrative over and over again. And then they use their ex-president to endorse the resistance. All to make them march, make them protest, make them scream racism and sexism and xenophobia and homophobia and smash windows, burn cars, shut down interstates and airports, bully and terrorize the law abiding—until the only option left is for police to do their jobs and stop the madness.

She called liberal rhetoric the "violence of lies" and recommended responding with the "clenched fist of truth." While there's a veneer of plausible deniability there, it's clear her insinuation was that violence against liberals is acceptable—and can even be considered "self-defense," because, uh, liberal "lies" are a form of violence.

This sort of thing is frustrating, because the liberal tendency, which I share in abundance, is to see a huge pile of bullshit like that and get to work trying to debunk it. Loesch's rhetoric is mostly lies, and when it's not, it's asserting racist and fascistic ideas—such as the notion that Obama should not be allowed to express his opinion. Or that it's not really his opinion, but something he was put up to by white liberals, which is a common accusation made by right wingers against people of color.

But really, trying to debunk such things piece by piece is missing the forest for the trees, especially since the audience for such debunkings, other liberals, can already see this nonsense for what it is. Instead, it's interesting to look at the function and purpose of these kinds of disinformation campaigns.

Why Loesch's bit of Goebbels-esque propaganda about socialists and cosmopolitans is ultimately a buy-more-guns message may not be apparent at first blush to people who aren't really interested in guns, i.e., most readers of this book. But advertising rarely works on the conscious and rational mind. Think of the last ad you saw on TV. Was it a direct pitch about the product's features and how you will find them useful? Or did it push a bunch of emotional buttons, often ones that had nothing to do with the product?

Honestly, it's easier to see the connection between Loesch's violent rhetoric and the buy-more-guns pitch than to understand why a chewing gum should remind you of your mother's love or an underarm deodorant should make you feel happier. She makes the conservative viewer feel angry and powerless, and buying guns are offered as a way to feel powerful and in control.

The NRA's representatives would deny it if you suggested that the message was to buy guns to shoot liberals. And it's probably fair to note that they don't really want conservatives to go light up an anti-Trump protest with an AR-15, if only because the media backlash would go badly for the NRA. But it is true that the NRA pushes a bunch of emotional buttons on the right and prescribes spending more money on guns as a way for conservatives to feel better.

The problem with this, beyond the ethical quandaries of treating the brothers in ideology like marks in the long-running con that is the gun industry, are twofold: One, this marketing strategy is fueling the right wing political derangement that elected Trump and is tearing this country apart. Two, all those guns being sold are leading to a whole bunch of unnecessary deaths.

Rhetoric of the sort dished out by Loesch is the single biggest reason that the United States is in the horrible predicament we're in now. Sociologists and historians will debate for years why so many suburban and rural white people were open to hearing these kinds of claims, but the one indisputable fact is that there is a cottage industry of people who are profiting off telling conservative America that they are facing some existential threat—and that violent, hateful rejection of everything liberals believe or even just like is the only appropriate response.

Vote for Trump and buy a gun: the two best ways a red-blooded American asshole can rattle liberals. The NRA themselves clearly saw the link between these two actions, spending over $30 million on promoting his candidacy alone in 2016, which more than doubles the $12.5 million they spent on Mitt Romney in 2012.

The irony here is that both choices—voting for Trump and buying a gun—often end up hurting the people who make them as much, if not more, than it hurts liberals.

With guns, the statistical evidence of this is unquestionable. All that gun-buying has made life in red America more dangerous. If you live in a community that has more guns per capita or more lax gun laws, you are more likely to be shot. It's not just because of murder, either. Suicide and accident rates are also higher for these communities.

Right wing media does what it can to distract from these facts. On Fox News and right wing talk radio, for instance, there's a lot of racist chatter about "black on black crime" and the murder rate in places like Chicago or Baltimore. This kind of rhetoric serves the dual purpose of making white conservatives fearful, so they buy more guns, and also portraying gun violence as a problem for "those" people, and not for your own.

But while urban crime is a problem, ultimately the issue still goes back to the overly lax gun laws in this country. As organizations like the Brady Campaign to Prevent Gun Violence have demonstrated repeatedly, every illegal gun used by a criminal to commit a crime started its life out as a legal gun. Cities can have all the gun laws they want, but if it's an hour drive away to a place where gun restrictions are few in number, then it's easy enough for black market dealers to buy a bunch of legal guns that they then sell illegally in the cities. There's a reason the NRA fights every effort to make it harder for straw buyers to bulk-buy guns to sell on the black market: The gun industry relies on those sales to pad out profits.

Plugging into the hate-the-liberals mentality of troll nation has been quite profitable in general for the gun industry. Even though the number of gun owners has gone down, the number of gun sales actually went up during the Obama administration. That's for a very simple reason: right wing nuts, angry over a black Democrat in the White House, bought into the idea that the way to ameliorate their bitterness was to buy more guns to cling to.

Nowadays, according to a Washington Post analysis, the average gun owner owns eight guns, twice the number that they did in the '90s.

Most guns range in price from $350 for a handgun to $1,000 for an assault rifle. The average gun-owning right wing nut now must spend thousands of dollars on an accessory collection that has no real purpose out of imagining how much it must aggravate the liberals, if they were ever to lay eyes on it. No wonder these are the same people who were credulous enough to vote for Trump.

Case Study: Sarah Palin

In mid-October 2017, Sen. John McCain—who enjoys being seen as one of the few Republicans who will stand up to Donald Trump, even though he doesn't do it as much as he'd like you to think—was awarded with the Liberty Medal from the National Constitution Center. He used his acceptance speech to blast Trump, though like fellow Republican coward George W. Bush, who made a similar speech, he did so without mentioning Trump's name.

In his speech, McCain denounced "half-baked, spurious nationalism cooked up by people who would rather find scapegoats than solve problems" and hinted that Trump was a wannabe fascist by saying America is "a land made of ideals, not blood and soil."

It was all very uplifting and got McCain a good deal of the fawning press he enjoys, but for those of us who have memories that extend years instead of months, McCain's self-congratulation was infuriating. McCain has never really admitted the role he played in the rise of troll nation, or the choices he made that helped usher in this new era of blood-and-soil conservatism that is more interested in pissing off liberals than in good governance.

It was McCain, after all, who picked Sarah "Blood and Soil" Palin to be his running mate in 2008. While Palin's fame isn't the sole cause of the situation the country finds itself in now, it's also undeniable that she helped enshrine the know-nothing trolling aesthetic that defines modern conservatism—and therefore paved the way for Trump's candidacy.

McCain likely picked Palin, then governor of Alaska, in a moment of weakness. The candidacy of Barack Obama, already historic and inspiring, had just hit a high moment at the Democratic National Convention. So many people showed up that they were forced to move to the Mile High Stadium on the last day, to accommodate the over 80,000 people that showed up for Obama's speech. Obama was a rock star, and so it wasn't hard to see why, the very day after Obama's speech, McCain snagged this woman whose good looks and folksy charm promised to steal a headline or two away from Obama.

Well, his choice was extremely effective at attracting media attention—but perhaps not in the way that McCain hoped. It soon became clear that Palin was some combination of intrinsically dumb and deeply incurious. She repeatedly humiliated herself in front of the press and during the vice presidential debate, when she failed to converse intelligently about even the most basic political issues.

Palin wasn't really about policy or governance. Instead, she was about promoting a very simple message: Rural, white Americans were the only Americans that count, and the rest of us were interlopers to be regarded with hostility and suspicion.

"We believe that the best of America is in these small towns that we get to visit, and in these wonderful little pockets of what I call the real America," she said in an October 2008, adding that they were "pro-America areas of this great nation" where "we find the kindness and the goodness and the courage"—very clearly indicating that people living in cities had none of these values.

When called out on it, she offered a mealy-mouthed apology, saying, "If that's the way it has come across, I apologize" to a CNN reporter.

Her attempt to pretend she was misunderstood was even more repulsive in light of her convention speech, given just a few days after McCain selected her as a running mate. This notion, that small town white people are the only people of value, was baked directly into that speech as well.

"A writer observed, 'We grow good people in our small towns, with honesty and sincerity and dignity,'" she said.

The quote caught a lot of attention, not just because of its unsavory implications, which later became blunt assertions with her "real America" talk, but because it's really unusual for politicians to quote someone in a speech anonymously. Usually, quoting writers is accompanied by telling people *what* writer you are quoting.

Diligent journalists quickly figured out the likely reason for the omission: the quote came from a 20th century writer named Westbrook Pegler, whose views were rabidly anti-union, incredibly racist and outright fascist. He was such a right wing radical that the John Birch Society fired him because of his extremist views. (He recommended that readers bat "the brains out of" striking workers, called Jews "geese," claimed it was "the bounden duty of all intelligent Americans to proclaim and practice bigotry," and hoped "some white patriot of the Southern tier will spatter [Robert Kennedy's] spoonful of brains in public premises before the snow flies"—a wish that came true 3 years later.)

It was widely believed that Palin's fatal mix of ignorance and fascistic rhetoric helped doom the already struggling McCain campaign. There's certainly some data to back this up, suggesting that the American brain rot that led to Trump's election was far from complete in 2008.

Still, it is undeniable that Palin excited a certain group of Republican voters that had previously been marginalized: ignorant, racist, mean-spirited, and downright nihilistic. Her presence on the trail made it clear that this group was a much bigger chunk of the conservative voting base than pundits, political consultants, politicians, and even the Palin base voters themselves had ever believed possible. And the more that journalists exposed her ignorance and pundits laughed at her idiocy, the more her base loved her. If the "liberal elite" hates her so much, troll nation thinks, she must be doing something right.

Crowds at McCain rallies swelled after they became McCain/Palin rallies, in a phenomenon that Politico deemed the "Palin effect." ABC News reported that McCain rallies, which were drawing about 1,000 people before, were growing in size, often topping over 10,000 people—in St. Louis, it even got to 17,000 people.

"I could not ask for a greater partner than the governor of Alaska, Sarah Palin," McCain declared to a New Mexico crowd. "Because the response, the response to her has been overwhelming, it's been incredible, she's ignited America. I'm so proud to have her with me."

It wasn't hard to see what Palin brought to the table. What she lacked in intelligence, she made up for in pandering to the worst kind of people. I got a taste of it myself that fall, while taking a walk through Austin, Texas, where I then lived. While most of the city is pretty liberal, there are still some angry red staters lingering around. One of my neighbors put up a Confederate flag in his yard, with a sign reading "I'm a mavrik, how about you?" accompanied by two signs with "socialest" and "Obama" with red slash marks through them. (Yes, those are the way they were spelled.)

I stopped to take a picture of this display and struck up a conversation with the elderly white people on the porch, asking them about the signs. They were eager to talk, gushing about how much they adored Palin. They never mentioned the actual presidential nominee, McCain, once.

After nominating Palin, things got ugly quickly for McCain. He kept vacillating for the rest of the campaign between indulging in Palin's nationalistic rhetoric and then, in moments of conscience, recoiling. The crowds turning out at Republican rallies kept getting meaner. The *New York Times* reported attendees shouting things like "kill him," "off with his head," and racial slurs about Obama.

At one rally, a woman came up to the microphone and said she could not trust Obama, because he's an "Arab." McCain, looking a bit ill, said, "No, ma'am, he's a decent family man, citizen who I just happen to have disagreements with on fundamental issues." Another man said he was "scared" of Obama, and when McCain disagreed, saying Obama is "a decent person," the crowd booed.

Palin had no such hesitation about wallowing in the worst impulses of the right, declaring at one rally that Obama enjoyed "palling around with terrorists." Her favorite catchphrase, "Drill, baby, drill," quickly became famous, as crowds, who likely had no ill will towards polar bears and other Alaskan wildlife before this, charged along. The slogan distilled a conservative ethos that whatever angers liberals—in this case, destroying the Artic ecosystem—is what conservatives need to be doing.

As soon as McCain lost and she was rid of the yoke of the 2008 election, Palin listlessly hung onto her Alaskan governorship for a few more months before quitting to do what she really loved: trolling liberals for money. She threw herself into speaking tours and publishing her half-written books, all of which riffed on the her favorite theme, which is that liberals suck and that one's life should be lived in pursuit of angering them.

"Liberals, you want to send those evil employees who would dare work at a fast food joint then ya just don't believe in, thought you wanted to, I dunno, send them to Purgatory or somethin' so they all go VEGAN and, uh, wages and picket lines I dunno they're not often discussed in Purgatory, are they," went one memorable 2014 rant from her online video network.

Or her description of Christmas 2012, in her book *Good Tidings and Great Joy: Protecting the Heart of Christmas*: "To combat the anti-gun chatter coming from Washington, I surprised [her husband, Todd] with a nice, needed, powerful gun."

She called it an act of "civil disobedience." Her Christmas joy, it's worth noting, was due to the recent murders of 26 people, 20 of whom were small children, at Sandy Hook Elementary School. Without that shooting, there wouldn't have been all that "anti-gun chatter" that winter that was so much *fun* for Palin to retaliate against.

(Dan Savage, who drew my attention to this passage, noted in his review that this passage "ends with Palin bragging about her tits," which I was sadly able to verify.)

Naturally, Palin was eager to inject herself into the Trump campaign and her reason was that he is just so damn good at angering those liberals. Her endorsement was announced by the Trump campaign, and her stream-of-consciousness speech did not disappoint people who take a macabre glee in watching Palin try to out-stupid herself.

"You know, it's really funny to me to see the 'splodey heads keep 'sploding over this movement," she said in the truly bizarre speech.

At least she appeared to mean metaphorical 'sploding. With all those liberal-aggravating guns around, there is always the danger of real human heads actually exploding.

Palin is a publicity hound and a born troll, but it quickly became clear that she was a mere amateur compared to the first rate trolls of Trump world. Her folksy sneering at the "liberal elite" felt a bit quaint compared to Trump's ability to spout racist vitriol, mock disabled people, and suggest openly that women's only value is sexual. Annoying liberals is a competitive sport, and Palin's insipid provocations, which had been so attention catching before, started to feel like bush league antics. She's still banging around out there, trying to con some money out of the rubes, but her star has dimmed considerably compared to Trump, who, when it comes to being an asshole, is the sun.

Chapter 7

Race

Of the many, many strange revelations that unfolded upon learning that the Russian government had interfered with the 2016 election, one of the weirdest was the way that Russian troll farms deliberately stoked already existing racial anxieties in the American public.

"Another Gruesome Attack on Police By A BLM Movement Activist" blared one Facebook ad, bought by Russian agents, and featuring a picture of a flag-draped coffin at a police funeral.

"Get Ready To Secede," screamed another, accompanied by menacing pictures of dark-skinned people, which was aimed at Texas conservatives.

Fake social media accounts run by Russian operatives claimed to see Black Lives Matter protesters burning flags. They organized rallies against immigration and in support of Confederate statues. In one hilarious case, they even tried to convince white conservatives that civil rights activists were opposed to Christmas.

In contrast, ads aimed at anti-racists were either bland—it's not entirely clear what Russia was trying to accomplish with basic ads stating police violence is wrong—or, more commonly, aimed at driving down voter turnout by spreading racially loaded false stories about the Clintons, such as an ad claiming Bill Clinton has a black son he won't acknowledge.

By and large, though, Russian operators bought ads meant to build on a larger propaganda effort run by homegrown right wing media and the Trump campaign. Many of these ads worked by playing on the racist themes Trump, and his supporters at outlets like Breitbart, were regularly pumping into the news cycle.

Republicans have long known that race-baiting is a useful way to snag the majority of white voters. It's a lot harder to win running on issues like cutting taxes for the rich or letting corporations poison your drinking water. Trump just dialed that strategy up, realizing that as long as he dished out race-baiting nonsense, the majority of white voters would forgive his incompetence and loutishness. If anything, they would love him more for these qualities. Yes, he may be a corrupt, soulless monster, but he was willing to put his evil to use enforcing unjust racial hierarchies, and that was just the kind of monster right wing voters wanted.

Of course, the one thing that remains true in American political life is that pretty much no one wants to be *called* a racist. Even white supremacists, before pulling on their Klan hoods or donning their Nazi gear, will whine that they're not racist, they're just for "white power" or against "white genocide" or think "white lives matter."

Trump himself will flip between calling white supremacists "fine people" or stoking yet another pointless racist controversy and sending his press secretary out to deny that he's racist. People rally around statues of men who literally started a war to defend slavery and claim that can't be racist, because of "heritage." It's a heritage of white supremacy defended by violence, but the use of the word "heritage" illustrates the kind of slipperiness that defines the discourse about race in this country. Even after witnessing hundreds of years of violence over the question of whether or not all people will be treated equally, many still act like "racism" is some minor bad habit of a few marginal people, instead of one of the defining struggles of American history.

For the members of troll nation, the efforts to perpetuate racism while denying racism create a politics of whiplash. One minute they're denouncing anti-racists as "snowflakes" who are too politically correct and easily offended. The very next moment, alt-rights are taking umbrage and having emotional meltdowns at the slightest hint of resistance to racial inequities in America.

I went over some of this territory in the chapters on political correctness, which covered how conservatives have managed to convince themselves that kneeling NFL players, for instance, are somehow both shivering snowflakes that need to toughen up and are doing something unbelievably offensive that needs to be censored immediately, to protect the paper-thin skin of conservatives. But that barely brushes the surface of what may be the most serious damage that troll nation has done to this country: reinvigorating old racial hatreds that were actually starting to be eroded, however slowly, in 21st century America.

Trump may not be the brightest bulb, but in his role as the cult leader of Trumpism, he has figured one thing out: the quickest way to reaffirm his connection to his base voters and maintain their loyalty is to attack people of color.

Trump has, at the time this book is being written, twice launched despicable public attacks on the bereaved families of soldiers of color lost in combat. That's the sort of thing that used to be inconceivable, no matter political party or ideology, but especially so for conservatives. It used to be believed that military duty and the attendant patriotic respect for it were untouchable values on the American right.

But this is the season of the troll, and even a gold standard conservative value like respect for the military has given way to the deeper need of right wing America to see someone hector the liberals and, more importantly, to sabotage efforts at racial diversity and equality in this country. Attacking these military families, who were visibly not white people, allowed Trump the space to redefine patriotism and military valor as white-only ideals. He could prove that he could do something as vile as belittle the pain of a grieving parent or spouse, and troll nation would still have his back. They may even like him a little better.

Trump famously tested these waters during the campaign, when Khizr and Ghazala Khan, the parents of U.S. Army Captain Humayun Khan, gave a speech at the Democratic National Convention. Captain Khan died during the Iraq War and was posthumously awarded a Bronze Star Medal and a Purple Heart, as well as burial in Arlington National Cemetery. The Clinton campaign had tapped the Khans to offer a rebuke to Trump's constant insinuations that Muslims could never be patriotic Americans. During the speech, Khizr Khan, who made a living as an attorney, whipped out his pocket constitution and powerfully denounced Trump's rejection of the constitutional guarantees of freedom of religion and equal protection under the law.

"Donald Trump, you are asking Americans to trust you with our future. Let me ask you: Have you even read the U.S. Constitution? I will gladly lend you my copy. In this document, look for the words 'liberty' and 'equal protection of law,'" Khan said, his emotion rising. "You have sacrificed nothing and no one."

Trump lashed back in a gross, racist attack on the Khans, where he suggested he had sacrificed as much as a lost son by creating "thousands of jobs," and by suggesting that Ghazala Khan "wasn't allowed to have anything to say" on stage.

At the time, the grotesque attack on what is known as a "Gold Star family" was widely viewed by pundits as a disaster for the Trump campaign, precisely because military service is viewed in such glowing terms in conservative circles. But in reality, the damage it did to Trump was, at best, temporary. His base continued to love him and didn't mind that he was such a cruel monster to these parents. It seems that, for many right wingers, the laudability of military service is dependent on the ethnicity of the soldier in question.

All of which is why I struggle to believe it was an accident that Trump went back to that well a little over a year later, in the fall of 2017. In the face of bad press over a fatal mission in Niger, the ongoing Russia investigation, and the daily outrage over the lies and the tweets, Trump managed to regain control over the news cycle in the ugliest way possible: He got into a public fight with the family and friends of Sgt. La David Johnson, a black soldier who died trying to save his colleague's life after ISIS-affiliated militants attacked a Green Beret working in the region.

Trump was publicly criticized about his condolence call to Johnson's pregnant widow, Myeshia Johnson, in which he reportedly forgot La David Johnson's name and then said, "He knew what he signed up for, but I guess it still hurt." Rep. Frederica Wilson, a black congresswoman from Florida, heard the call on speakerphone while riding with Johnson's family in a limo. She was the first to talk about it to reporters, but both Johnson's mother and widow agreed publicly to her accounting of it.

The attack on Rep. Wilson and the surviving relatives of Sgt. Johnson was just as bad, if not worse than what Trump launched against the Khans. He repeatedly accused Myeshia Johnson of lying, even as photos of the pregnant woman crying over her husband's coffin kept flashing onscreen on cable news shows. He deputized his chief of staff, John Kelly, to lie about Rep. Wilson, falsely accusing her of taking credit for fundraising in a speech in which she did no such thing. No matter how many times the press disproved Kelly's account, however, he refused to apologize to Rep. Wilson.

These two stories are probably well known to the reader, but worth repeating here because they're a dramatic illustration of the depths to which troll nation has sunk. Trump's and Kelly's public confidence in the attacks on these Gold Star families isn't just an act meant to cow the media criticism. They are quite aware that the rabidly right wing, nastily racist base doesn't care about evidence or even very basic values like empathy and human decency. If anything, attacking the integrity of soldiers of color pleases the darkest impulses of the modern American right, and their belief that it's better to tear our country apart rather than accept the premise that a black or Muslim soldier has the same value as a white Christian one.

Historically, *Slate* writer Jamelle Bouie wrote, "the mere fact of black soldiers challenged ideals of American manhood and citizenship that were built on whiteness. To take up arms in defense of the nation was both an obligation of citizenship and a privilege rightfully reserved for white men."

It was hoped, of course, that those attitudes were in the past. The grim truth that Trump has unearthed, unfortunately, is that they were not nearly as past as thought. It may be that Trump just lashed out at criticism, especially when it comes from people he sees, because of their ethnicity, as lesser than him. But it also may be that he has tapped into something very real and very ugly in the soul of conservative America. Nothing says a rejection of full citizenship for non-white people more than refusing to offer them the same respect for military service that white people get.

To be clear, there's nothing new about race-baiting for Republican candidates. If anything, the Republican party, in its current form, exists because of racism. The "Southern strategy" was developed by Richard Nixon in the '60s to capitalize on white Southerners abandoning the Democratic Party in droves, after Lyndon B. Johnson signed the Civil Rights Act into law.

This isn't a hidden history. Many, many, many people—including myself—have quoted Republican operative Lee Atwater's famously frank 1981 interview where he said, "You start out in 1954 by saying, 'N—er, n—er, n—r.' By 1968 you can't say 'n—er'—that hurts you, backfires. So you say stuff like, uh, forced busing, states' rights, and all that stuff, and you're getting so abstract. Now, you're talking about cutting taxes, and all these things you're talking about are totally economic things and a byproduct of them is, blacks get hurt worse than whites."

If there's any single principle that troll nation stands for, it's running away from that process Atwater described, of softening and abstracting racism. Instead they are returning, if not to using the infamous N-word, at least towards blunter, more overtly racist rhetoric and posturing.

Republicans did this to themselves. For decades, conservative pundits have made a bogeyman out of "political correctness," telling their audiences that being expected to speak politely and curtail one's most bigoted impulses in public is a form of oppression and may even be a violation of their free speech. People who blanch at racist or sexist rhetoric are characterized as "snowflakes" or told they're "playing the victim."

After all those years attacking liberals for political correctness, there would come a time when Republican voters started noticing that their own party also lived by the rule that there are just some ideas that are socially unacceptable to utter. The process that Atwater is describing, where conservatives adjust their rhetoric over time to make it sound less bigoted, is nothing if not its own kind of political correctness.

Paul Ryan's policies, for instance, may achieve racist ends, but he mostly shies away from the red meat rhetoric explicitly demonizing racial minorities as criminals or welfare queens. That's why the word "cuck"—a nasty term, drawn from porn, suggesting a man is emasculated—is used by the alt-right to describe not liberals, but mostly mainstream conservatives that they see as weak and placating to the forces of "political correctness."

The theory that is widespread in troll nation is that everyone (everyone white, anyway) is racist, and anyone who doesn't act that way is putting on an act. Trump's relative willingness to spout off racist nonsense, therefore, reads as refreshingly honest. That most of what he says is false doesn't change this belief in his honesty. His supporters see in him a permission structure to let loose with the venom they feel has been unfairly suppressed by those mean liberals and all their concerns about people's feelings—well, people besides right wing bigots' feelings, anyway. The hurt feelings of a bigot who dislikes being called a racist is always, in these circles, considered a genuine pain that deserves compassion.

The shift in conservative media towards troll nation's way of doing business can be seen during the 8 PM Eastern Standard Time slot on Fox News. It's a slot that used to be occupied by Bill O'Reilly, but when O'Reilly was fired due to an advertising boycott brought on by revelations about the millions the network had paid to multiple women in sexual harassment settlements, Tucker Carlson took over the seat.

Both men, let it be said, are extremely racist. Much of O'Reilly's show was dedicated to the message that criminal and oversexed black people were ruining America. He often ran alarmist stories on whatever rapper he thought would most scare his elderly white audience that week. He defended the shooting of Trayvon Martin, an unarmed teenager, because the young man was wearing a hoodie, saying Martin would have been safe if he had, no joke, worn a jacket and a tie to go to the corner store for candy. O'Reilly even once marveled that there's "no difference between Sylvia's restaurant," a famous Harlem institution, "and any other restaurant in New York City," even "though it's run by blacks, primarily black patronship."

O'Reilly got downright hysterical on repeated occasions about the popularity of Beyoncé, whining about the song "Drunk in Love," which he claimed was irresponsible because "young girls are getting pregnant in the African American community" and that it's "70 percent out of wedlock." The cynical racism of this particular rant is obvious enough to anyone who has actually heard the song and knows it's literally about a married couple's date night, and knows that the video features Beyoncé's real life husband, Jay-Z. But O'Reilly likely knew that his audience, nearly all-white and of the average age of 70, would know nothing about the song, except that it was sung by a black woman and they don't like that one bit.

So let it be known that O'Reilly is a human garbage can. Still, Carlson somehow found a way to build on O'Reilly's cheap, attention-grabbing race-baiting by marrying it to the pseudo-intellectualism and victim complex that defines the alt-right. O'Reilly is a racist, but Carlson is even closer to a white national-ist. Carlson's short stint on the network is notable mostly for the work he does to mainstream white nationalist claims, five hours a week for an audience of millions.

Carlson is too smart to promote white nationalism directly. Instead, his strategy is to portray the far right as victims of cen-sorship and political correctness. His pose is to avoid mentioning the content of white nationalist beliefs. Instead, he argues that he's defending their right to a hearing, which he claims they don't get, due to all this mythical liberal censorship. He couples this with segments portraying critics of white nationalism as the "real" radicals who are a threat to the country.

A recent example involving the website Gab provides a good illustration. Gab is pretty clearly a white supremacist site, even though, like most white supremacists, they like to play dumb about this fact in public. The site was started as a social media platform for those who are too toxic and bigoted for Twitter—which is really saying something, because Twitter is notorious for doing very little to control the neo-Nazi infestation that plagues the microblogging network. Gab's logo is even a green frog face, a conspicuous nod to the use of frog imagery that white supremacists adopted during the Trump campaign.

(There are many explainers online about why white supremacists are into frogs. No need to get into the details here. Just suffice it to say: they like frog pictures.)

In his segment on Gab, however, Carlson mentioned none of this. Instead, he posited that a private company like Google somehow has no right to deny Gab access to its online store to recruit users, arguing that Google was employing "arbitrary hate speech policies."

The word "arbitrary" sounds good and scary, but there was nothing arbitrary about Google's decision at all. What Carlson skipped mentioning was that Gab is full of unapologetic neo-Nazis and vicious bigots. Refusing to host a site that deliberately attracts neo-Nazis is the opposite of arbitrary. "No Nazis" is the soul of a clear, understandable decency standard.

But that's how Carlson works: He gets a headful of umbrage at what he deems unfair attacks on white nationalists and neo-Nazis, which allows him to portray these people in a sympathetic light without having to defend the content of their ideas.

One of Carlson's favorite tactics is to invite critics of white nationalism as guests and then hold them up as hate objects for his conservative audience. I myself was once targeted by this strategy. I had written a piece for Salon criticizing Trump for a speech he gave in Poland, where he openly pandered to the European far-right with rhetoric echoing white supremacist talking points that imply that only people of European heritage have created great art or made important scientific discoveries.

Shortly after I published this article, I got an email from Carlson's producer, blandly asking me on his show to discuss my ideas. And while I, like most journalists who have websites to promote, usually jump at the opportunity to talk about my work with an audience of millions, I've seen enough of Carlson's show to know what the game was: They'd bring me on, knowing that his audience would immediately peg me as educated, feminist, and urbane—and therefore an uppity bitch. Even if I showed up wearing a kitten sweater and a giant gold cross necklace, the show would likely have a chyron identifying me as a member of the "liberal elite." Then Carlson would spend a few minutes asking dumb questions and talking to me like I'm obviously an idiot. Even if you've got the rhetorical talents of Martin Luther King, good luck, under those circumstances, trying to look like anything but the broad stereotype Carlson wants you to be.

The game Carlson is playing is simple: Set the liberal up as a hate object, and make the people who the liberal is criticizing—whether it's Trump or white supremacists—seem sympathetic in comparison. Rather than play the heel in a morality play about how liberals are big meanies for criticizing white supremacy, I took a pass.

Unsurprisingly, Carlson's effective strategy at making white supremacists look like the good guys has made his show a huge hit with the white supremacist crowd. Online forums dedicated to promoting white nationalism have adopted the motto, "You can't cuck the Tuck!"

"This guy used to be the worst type of bowtie wearing faggot," neo-Nazi Andrew Anglin, who hosts the Third Reich-celebrating site Daily Stormer wrote. "Oh but now—this man is a machine of ultimate destruction."

Anglin also praises Carlson as the neo-Nazis' "greatest ally" and takes special pleasure in watching Carlson go after Jewish guests, calling him a "one-man HOLOCAUST."

"He doesn't even attack Hitler," Anglin once marveled, a man in love.

Notorious former Klansman and current white supremacist David Duke is also a big fan of what he sees as Carlson's anti-Semitic agenda, declaring that Carlson sticks it to "Jewish supremacists."

Carlson's show isn't just a huge hit with the open Nazis, sadly. His is usually the first or second-highest rated cable news show in any given month, pulling in 2.5 to 3 million viewers nightly, even as he winks and nods to white supremacists. Many of these viewers would probably reject white supremacist ideas if presented to them straightforwardly. Carlson is winning them over with "enemy of my enemy" arguments.

After all, just like mainstream conservatives, white supremacists also hate "political correctness," liberal college professors, and hot feminists who look at you like your dick is made of bees. And so Carlson slowly convinces them to like white supremacists a little more every day. If trolling liberals makes your heart sing, well, no one angers liberals better than a neo-Nazi.

This kind of bankshot argument, where racist ideas are advanced by demonizing anti-racists as the "liberal elite," is no longer just about abstract culture war fights. It's being used to advance policies that are directly harming some of the most vulnerable people in the country: undocumented immigrants.

The story begins, as these things often do, in the most innocuous of ways. For a few years now, local police departments have, after being repeatedly burned by Immigration and Customs Enforcement (ICE) pushing them to make decisions that were counter-productive to their crime fighting priorities, started fighting back. Local police departments in cities across the country started telling ICE they weren't going to hold people suspected of being undocumented without legal cause, especially since some cities had been sued for doing this to people who were, it was later revealed, legal residents or even citizens. Some police departments also resisted ICE's efforts to inject themselves into ordinary police work, like taking witness statements, correctly pointing out that when communities hate and fear the cops, it makes it harder for the police to do their jobs.

These choices weren't really made out of noble anti-racist intentions, but more because police departments were sick of being deputized to do ICE's work for them. Conservatives, however, saw a golden opportunity for some demagoguery and came up with the term "sanctuary cities" to describe any city that had police resistant to doing ICE's job for them.

It was, unfortunately, genius branding. It's not just that the term falsely implied that cities were offering actual sanctuary to undocumented immigrants who are worried about deportation. (ICE can still choose to deport people, even if local police refuse to cooperate with their efforts.) It's that the term "sanctuary city" invokes an immediate narrative for conservative audiences: Liberal elites, in a bout of well-intended naiveté, are flouting the law and are giving sanctuary to these immigrants, who thank those soft-hearted liberals by raping and murdering them.

It's yet another example of how the political correctness narrative is really a vehicle for racist sentiments, such as claiming an inherent criminality to non-white immigrants, that can't be voiced directly. (Though, in the age of Trump, just calling immigrants a bunch of criminals has become more acceptable than it used to be.) Instead, the supposed objects of the criticism are not the immigrants, but the elitist white liberals who foolishly coddle immigrants. This way, conservatives can look like they are punching up, by attacking educated white urban liberals, rather than punching down.

Trolling educated white liberals is always a good game, in no small part because there's a contingent of educated white liberals, particularly men, who kind of buy into this idea that urban white liberals are effete wimps, and that "heartland" whites are somehow more manly and authentic. And so these anxious liberals are eager to show how down they are with the pickup truck crowd by scolding each other for supposedly looking down their nose at the simple-minded, honest folk of middle America, who are held in high honor by people who seem to think middle Americans are too dumb to know that racism is wrong.

(This kind of condescension always strikes me as more obnoxious than the moral disapproval other urban liberals are accused of offering our Republican-voting fellow Americans, but what do I know? I'm actually from rural Texas, and my opinions on my own people do not count.)

The way this whole game works was captured nicely in the Virginia governor's race in 2017. The Republican candidate, Ed Gillespie, decided to run a very Trump-like campaign against the Democrat, Ralph Northam, who served as lieutenant governor under Gov. Terry McAuliffe.

Even though there are no "sanctuary cities" in Virgina, Gillespie decided to make sanctuary cities, as well as Confederate statues, a major issue in his race. He ran ads decrying Northam's alleged support for sanctuary cities while flashing a menacing picture of members of MS-13—a picture literally taken in an El Salvadoran prison, not anywhere in Virginia.

MS-13 is a real gang, but that's all that can really be said to be true about Gillespie's campaign strategy. The reality is crime has been in decline in the past few years in Virginia, as in most of the country, and Virginia has a low crime rate compared to its neighboring states. There are no "sanctuary cities" in Virginia, but even if there were, it doesn't actually mean, despite conservative hints to the contrary, that criminals are allowed to roam free. If you commit a crime like stealing or murder in a sanctuary city, you are still subject to criminal penalties, regardless of your immigration status. Gillespie was rolling out plain old race-baiting, but he did it by framing it as a problem of white liberals like Northam of being too politically correct to deal with the problem.

The good news is that, after a year of dealing with Trumpism, Gillespie's strategy backfired. He was able to turn out the same rural Virginia whites that voted for Trump, but suburban white Democrats, both moderate and progressive, turned out in droves to vote for Northam. They were sick, it seems, of being told they are stupid elitists who don't know what's good for them. Black voters, also sick of being treated like hate objects instead of full citizens, also turned out for Northam. It seems that the politics of culture war can swing both ways, at least some of the time.

While things worked out okay in the Virginia governor's race the battle over sanctuary cities has created the pretense for some terrible legislation in other states. Republican-led state legislatures are using the concept as a way to pass laws stripping Democratic-led cities of their local law enforcement control and forcing local police to do even more intrusive and counter-productive work for ICE. Texas, for instance, passed SB4, which not only requires local police to abide by all manner of ICE requests, but also allows police the right to demand proof of citizenship from anyone they think looks undocumented. Which, of course, is just legalized racial profiling, since the cops aren't likely to go after people they think might be Canadians overstaying a visa.

This sort of thing really gets at the heart of why troll nation is so dangerous. The politics of resentment—against wealthy NFL players or white liberals deemed "elite"—may seem on its surface to be relatively harmless. Annoying, sure, but these targets are relatively privileged and can handle a bunch of provincial suburban and rural trolls taking potshots at them.

But really, the whole thing is cover for a darker agenda, aimed directly at more vulnerable people. Attacks on NFL players are using rich athletes to conceal the real targets: ordinary black men and women subject to police violence. Attacks on well-off liberal cities deemed "sanctuary cities" are made to look like criticisms of the liberal elite, but they're actually cover for an assault on the human rights of immigrants, many of whom are here because they are fleeing poverty or violence back home. That's how troll nation works. They paint themselves as noble warriors against a politically correct elite, but in truth, their efforts are all aimed at hurting people who are already marginalized in American society.

Case Study: Greg Gianforte

On May 24, 2017, Greg Gianforte, the Republican candidate running to be a congressman from Montana, body-slammed a reporter for the *Guardian*, named Ben Jacobs, for asking him a question. Gianforte wanted to fill the seat left by Rep. Ryan Zinke when he became Interior Secretary under Trump. Jacobs had shown up at a campaign event and, recorder in hand, asked Gianforte a question about the cost of the Republican health care plan. At this point, Gianforte decided to send Jacobs to the emergency room.

Gianforte, who apparently remembered Jacobs for his previous reporting on Gianforte's financial ties to Russian companies that had been sanctioned by the U.S. government, became irate.

"I'm sick and tired of you guys," Gianforte can be heard saying on the tape. "Get the hell out of here. Get the hell out of here. The last guy did the same thing."

Outraged at reporters daring to ask questions of congressional candidates, Gianforte, in front of witnesses, grabbed Jacobs and threw him to the ground, breaking his glasses. Gianforte eventually pled guilty to misdemeanor assault, and, because he was running as a Republican in the troll nation era, the body-slamming jackass won anyway.

Liberals and journalists were outraged. But right wing America had a different interpretation, arguing that Jacobs was lying and also that Jacobs was asking for it. That these two stances seem to contradict each other—how can someone have "asked for" something that didn't happen?—didn't really seem to matter.

Gianforte's campaign staff mostly adopted the "he was lying" approach, releasing a statement claiming that Jacobs "grabbed

130

Greg's wrist, and spun away from Greg, pushing them both to the ground." The candidate also lied to the police about the incident, using the same line about wrist-grabbing and trying to argue that Jacobs was out of line for asking a question in the first place. He also whined to the police that the "liberal media" is "trying to make a story."

Ryu Spaeth of the *New Republic* argued that Gianforte's behavior was the result of the "Trump effect," both because of Gianforte's hostility—shared by Trump—to the free press, and in the shamelessness of using "bullying, delegitimization, and outrage" in an effort to discredit a truthful story.

But many in the conservative media thought this assault was a perfect opportunity to take an ideology built around trolling liberals to the next level, by encouraging conservatives to see Gianforte's violence as justified and manly.

"Did anyone get his lunch money stolen today and then run to tell the recess monitor?" Fox News regular Laura Ingraham tweeted. It's worth noting that the man she painted as an overreacting tattletale had to be rushed to the hospital after the attack to make sure he wasn't badly hurt.

Rush Limbaugh praised Gianforte for being a "manly, studly Republican" and accused Jacob of being a "pajama-clad journalist" who was "being insolent and disrespectful and whiny and moany and accusatory." (Accusing a man of wearing pajamas is right wing code for saying they're emasculated. No, I'm not kidding.)

"Let's ask why on Earth a House candidate in Montana should have to answer questions from a reporter for a BRITISH newspaper????" asked Tim Graham of Newsbusters. Jacobs is a reporter for the *Guardian US*, an American newspaper that is owned, as is Fox News, by a British media company.

"Jacobs is an obnoxious, dishonest first class jerk. I'm not surprised he got smacked," tweeted conservative pundit Brent Bozell.

No wonder Gianforte won his election. Jacobs works for a left-leaning newspaper, which means he has two strikes against him—being liberal and being a journalist—in right wing eyes. The whole incident shows physical violence and defamation are on the table, as far as troll nation is concerned, in the war on both liberals and truth itself.

Interestingly, the weight of the eyewitness testimony and the audio recording of the event caused Gianforte to cave in the weeks after the assault. He admitted in an apology letter sent to Jacobs a couple of weeks after the incident, "Notwithstanding anyone's statements to the contrary, you did not initiate any physical contact with me, and I had no right to assault you."

But shortly after sending that letter, Gianforte and his team slid right back into the trolling mentality, reverting to habit by saying clearly false things. In November, the police report—which shows Gianforte lying to detectives—was released to the Associated Press. When contacted by reporters about this, Gianforte's spokesman said, "no one was misled" by the statement Gianforte gave in which he clearly said untrue things about the assault to the police.

Jacobs and his lawyers immediately sent a cease-and-desist letter to Gianforte, demanding he and his team stop issuing "false and defamatory" statements about the assault.

Even before all this happened, Gianforte was a politician in the Trump mold. He has a history of ties to white supremacists, starting with his ties to Doug Wilson, an Idaho pastor who wrote a 1996 pamphlet titled "Southern Slavery, As It Was." In it, Wilson argues that slavery was "a life of plenty, of simple pleasures, of food, clothes, and good medical care" and "one could argue that the black family has never been stronger than it was under slavery."

Gianforte was on the board of the Association of Classical and Christian Schools, which Wilson founded, and is on the record praising Wilson for his "vision."

In 2016, the Southern Poverty Law Center issued a lengthy report about the troublingly high levels of support Montana Republicans had offered to a white nationalist named Taylor Rose. One of the prominent supporters was Gianforte, who, along with his wife, donated $340 to Rose's thankfully failed run for the state legislature.

When asked why he supported a white supremacist for the state legislature, Gianforte dismissed the question by saying, "I was unaware of some of his views and we supported him because we supported all (Republican) candidates in the last election."

Why it is that all these white supremacists so easily fit into mainstream Republicanism is a question pointedly ignored, not just by Gianforte, but by all Republicans who play the same game with Trump's repeated pandering to white supremacists.

Gianforte also embraces the kind of crank views that have unfortunately become viewed as normal Republican politics. For instance, the Huffington Post reported that Gianforte gave a speech in 2015 in which he denounced, of all things, letting elderly people retire, rather than expecting them to work until they drop dead.

"There's nothing in the Bible that talks about retirement," Gianforte sneered to an audience of alleged Christians at the Montana Bible College. Noting that Noah was supposedly 600 when he built the ark and not "cashing Social Security checks,"

he argued that the folks at the retirement home "have an obligation to work."

You'd think that Republicans, whose voting base tends to be
elderly and relatively well-off, would know better than to bash the
concept of retirement. But the nihilism of the modern day right
wing has metastasized and is growing, consuming everything
in sight. Liberals generally support Social Security, so it must,
by the logic of troll nation, be a program for a bunch of lazy,
worthless leeches who need to be put to work. Being able to enjoy
some time off after a lifetime of hard work sounds suspiciously
like something one of those do-gooder liberals would advocate,
so they're against it. And if you ask hard questions about those
views, be careful, because you might get body-slammed for your
efforts.

Chapter 8

Conspiracy Theories

In December 2016, 28-year-old Edgar Maddison Welch drove up from his home in North Carolina to Washington D.C.'s Comet Ping Pong, a kid-friendly pizzeria that doubles as a concert venue on some nights. Welch marched into the pizzeria around 3 in the afternoon, armed with an AR-15 assault rifle, a Colt 45 pistol, and 29 rounds of ammunition around his chest. The restaurant, which had children eating inside, was evacuated in a panic. At one point Welch, clearly on edge, ended up pointing his gun at an employee. Eventually, Welch fired shots at a locked closet door, destroying some computer equipment inside. In March of 2017, Welch pled guilty to weapons and assault charges.

The strangest part of this entire story was that Welch had, it seems, convinced himself to brandish a gun where kids were eating in order to "save" children. For Welch was a believer in a conspiracy theory that the alt-right had dubbed "Pizzagate."

Pizzagate believers argued that this particular restaurant was running a child sex ring in its basement and that Hillary Clinton and her campaign chairman, John Podesta, were avid participants in the systemic rape and kidnapping of children. Welch claimed he was there to "investigate" the claims.

"Raiding a pedo ring, possible [sic] sacrificing the lives of a few for the lives of many," Welch wrote in a text message to a friend. "Standing up against a corrupt system that kidnaps, tortures and rapes babies and children in our own back yard."

The shooting was the inevitable development of what has been an increasingly important part of the culture of troll nation: conspiracy theories. Truth and facts simply don't matter very much to conservatives in this era of right wing nihilism. The cause of attacking and destroying liberalism has become so all-consuming that reality itself is seen as little more than an obstacle to be overcome. Telling lies, even outrageous lies, is justified so long as it's in service of this mission to ruin liberals.

To be fair, there's nothing new about conspiracy theories in politics—and the left has sadly generated their own fair share of them. The 9/11 truther movement, which holds that George W. Bush deliberately brought down the Twin Towers in order to justify the Iraq War, started off in liberal circles. JFK assassination conspiracy theories also seemed to begin in liberal circles and are still occasionally believed by people on the left.

But the truth of the matter is that conservatism has a much bigger and broader problem with conspiracy theories, and has had this problem for a long time now. In fact, the right is so in tune with conspiracy theories that many of those that start on the left—including 9/11 trutherism, anti-vaccination conspiracy theories, and even JFK assassination theories—tend now to be as, if not more, popular in right wing than in left wing circles.

In the 1950s, the John Birch Society and Sen. Joseph McCarthy peddled claims that there was a widespread communist conspiracy to take over the government, which led to accusations against multiple innocent people at the State Department of being in on this conspiracy. The John Birch Society also perpetrated the notion that drinking water fluoridation was a communist mind control conspiracy.

In 1972, a book called *None Dare Call It Conspiracy* was published by Gary Allen and sold over 4 million copies. In it, Allen argues that an international conspiracy of feminists, environmentalists, anti-war activists, the United Nations, and even the Rockefellers were involved in a communist conspiracy channeled through the Council on Foreign Relations. This, in turn, morphed into the conspiracy theories about the "New World Order" that helped fuel the militia movement in the '90s that led to Timothy McVeigh bombing the Oklahoma City federal building in 1995.

Allen's theories gave birth to what is likely the most popular conspiracy theory in modern America that climate change is a hoax. It's a conspiracy theory that is believed by the majority of Republican voters and held up, to one degree or another, by nearly all Republican politicians, including Donald Trump.

The idea that climate change is a hoax has been around so long that most politicians and pundits can get away without stating it plainly and rather gesturing at it, claiming there's "doubt" about the science, which allows them to sound reasonable while still promoting this ridiculous idea. But when it was first formed, the theory was that the international communist cabal had created this hoax as a way to undermine capitalism. And to this day, if you press believers in the conspiracy theory about why they think that there's still "doubt" about the scientific consensus, many will admit to believing that they think scientific certainty in climate change stems not from an assessment of the scientific evidence, but from ideological hostility to capitalism. In other words, scientists are part of Gary Allen's communist conspiracy.

The irony here is that there's no small amount of projection going on. Conservatives are reflexively anti-liberal, and so accuse environmentalists of being reflexively anti-capitalist. Conservatives are protecting the money interests of oil and coal companies, and so turn around and claim scientists are getting paid to lie by agencies issuing grant money.

The Clintons, of course, have been favorite targets of right wing conspiracy theorists ever since Bill Clinton first ran for president. Unfortunately, the relentless drumbeat of accusations of murder, fraud, and various other conspiracies against the couple played a major role in the 2016 election. Gullible mainstream media outlets just kept getting lulled into believing that so much smoke *must* mean fire, and so kept running stories about "questions" regarding Benghazi, Clinton's email server, Clinton's health, or the Clinton Foundation—even though responsible and repeated investigations showed there was literally no illegal activity going on. But the right wing noise machine worked. By getting so many stories about "questions" into the headlines, they were able to create the suggestion that corruption was there, even though corruption continues not to be there.

The escalation of conspiracy theories about Hillary Clinton during the campaign is part of a larger trend, though, of conspiracy theories dominating the right wing imagination and crowding out any interest whatsoever in the boring old truth. There's been a decline in audience interest in right wing news outlets that have, in the past at least, felt some responsibility to stick to the facts. Outlets like Infowars—which features radio show host Alex Jones ranting about Pizzagate and how the Sandy Hook Elementary School shooting was a false flag operation—have grown in popularity. Breitbart, while it doesn't go as far as Infowars, hints at popular right wing conspiracy theories on a regular basis. And perhaps most importantly, social media has become a huge conduit for conspiracy theories, as both alt-righters with no moral compass and Russian propagandists pump out a regular stream of nonsensical stories geared towards demonizing liberals and creating a general attitude of paranoia and distrust in empirical fact among conservatives.

But there's almost no bigger mainstreamer of conspiracy theories than Trump himself. It always bears remembering that Trump's entire political career is a direct outgrowth of his enthusiasm for conspiracy theories. (And racism.) Trump had floated the idea of getting into politics and even running for office before Barack Obama became president, but it wasn't until a black man took an office that racists think no black person should ever have that Trump actually started injecting himself regularly into the political punditry game—and he did it with a conspiracy theory.

In the spring of 2011, Trump started heavily pushing the idea that Obama was not born in Hawaii, but was, as conspiracy theorists claimed, actually born in Kenya and had faked his birth certificate. Trump claimed on *Today* that he had hired investigators to go to Hawaii to find out the truth and "they cannot believe what they're finding."

This is almost certainly a lie—another example of conspiracy theorist projection. During the campaign, multiple journalists

139

confronted Trump about this claim, and he would usually deflect, saying, "the time isn't right" or "it's not appropriate now" to discuss his claims about Obama's birth. The Hawaii state registrar had no evidence of anyone hired by Trump coming by with inquiries.

"He's spent millions of dollars trying to get away from this issue," Trump said on Fox News in March 2011. "Millions of dollars in legal fees trying to get away from this issue." The evidence for this came directly out of Trump's ass.

"Now, somebody told me," Trump told Laura Ingraham that same month, "that where it says 'religion,' it might have 'Muslim.' And if you're a Muslim, you don't change your religion, by the way."

After Obama, frustrated by all this, released his long form birth certificate to the public, Trump kept at it, claiming, "A lot of people do not think it was an authentic certificate" and that "his mother was not in the hospital" on CNN. Repeatedly, he told reporters that Obama used to say he was born in Kenya, all of which is flatly untrue.

"In debate, @MittRomney should ask Obama why autobiography states 'born in Kenya, raised in Indonesia," Trump tweeted in October 2012.

In reality, Obama's memoir, "Dreams from My Father," explicitly notes, repeatedly, that he was born in Hawaii.

Trump also, as noted in the intro, floated the idea that Obama had faked his grades to get into Ivy League schools. He also suggested that Obama was flat-out lying about attending Columbia, telling the Conservative Political Action Conference in 2011, "The people that went to school with him, they never saw him, they don't know who he is. It's crazy."

"I remember often eating breakfast with Barack at Tom's Restaurant on Broadway," Phil Boerner, Obama's college roommate at Columbia, told the *New York Times* in 2009. "Occasionally we went to The West End for beers." He provided some photos of Obama, dressed in '80s-style coats and turtlenecks.

"Barack Obama '83 became the first College alumnus to be elected President of the United States," the university proudly announced in 2008.

Conspiracy theories about Obama continue to haunt Trump's imagination as president. On March 4, 2017, Trump launched a new conspiracy theory during his morning toilet-and-tweet ritual, where he multitasks by simultaneously eliminating the overcooked steak he consumed the night before and sowing lies and discord through social media. (It's the most productive he is all day, I suppose.)

"Terrible! Just found out that Obama had my 'wires tapped' in Trump Tower just before the victory. Nothing found. This is McCarthyism!" he tweeted at 6:35 AM.

"Is it legal for a sitting President to be 'wire tapping' a race for president prior to an election? Turned down by court earlier. A NEW LOW!" he tweeted at 6:49 AM.

"I'd bet a good lawyer could make a great case out of the fact that President Obama was tapping my phones in October, just prior to Election!" he tweeted at 6:52 AM.

"How low has President Obama gone to tapp [sic] my phones during the very sacred election process. This is Nixon/Watergate. Bad (or sick) guy!" he tweeted at 7:02 AM. Thankfully, after that, the presidential bowels had finished moving and the nation was spared any further bullshit on his Twitter account that morning.

The whole thing created a stink, both in the White House bathroom and in the world at large, as the media rushed around to figure out what the hell he was talking about, and Trump's staff tried to concoct some kind of bullshit excuse for why Trump's obvious lies were somehow "true," at least if you stood on your head, squinted, and gave up on any remaining hope for our democracy. Months later, the Justice Department wrote a court filing that made it clear that Trump Tower was never wiretapped.

The *New York Times* reported in November 2017 that Trump continues to use "closed-door conversations to question the authenticity of President Barack Obama's birth certificate."

Trump's already existing enthusiasm for conspiracy theories goes into overdrive every time new stories surface indicating that it's quite likely that he and his campaign were colluding with the Russian government to rat-fuck Hillary Clinton in 2016. For instance, Trump sent off the tweets accusing Obama of wiretapping him in the midst of a flurry of news coverage indicating that Trump's attorney general, Jeff Sessions, had lied during his confirmation hearing about his meeting with the Russian ambassador at a campaign event.

Similarly, as indictments came down against Trump campaign team members, including campaign manager Paul Manafort, in the fall of 2017, Trump started spewing conspiracy theories about Clinton left and right on Twitter, claiming that she had "rigged" the primaries and that she had somehow done something illegal by funding opposition research about him during the campaign.

But while Trump uses conspiracy theories strategically, there's reason to believe he's just a really big fan of them in general. It's arguable, in fact, that Trump's infamous speech kicking off his campaign was based on a conspiracy theory. In it, he literally argued that Mexico is "sending" people "that have lots of problems," people who are supposedly drug dealers and rapists, suggesting that there was a Mexican political conspiracy against the U.S. It wasn't just a figure of speech. On Twitter, Trump has repeatedly suggested that Mexico is deliberately unloading people their government doesn't want to deal with into the United States.

Similarly, Trump has suggested that ISIS is deliberately smuggling terrorists into the United States through the Syrian refugee program. This is a particularly dumb conspiracy theory, as the people who come in through the program undergo two years worth of vetting, and it's well-documented that ISIS prefers to recruit by appealing to lost young men that already live in Western countries through online propaganda.

Trump spent much of the 2016 campaign floating all manner of conspiracy theories. He suggested that Ted Cruz's father conspired to assassinate JFK. He told the *Washington Post* that he believed the death of Vince Foster, a Clinton aide who committed suicide in 1993, was "very fishy," adding, "He knew everything that was going on, and then all of a sudden he committed suicide." He suggested vaccines cause autism during a debate. He hinted to radio host Michael Savage that Justice Antonin Scalia was murdered. He claimed ISIS had sent a man to attack him, which did not happen. He suggested that the New York attorney general had been bribed to investigate a fraud Trump was sponsoring, in which people were conned out of money with false promises of a real estate education.

When the *Washington Post* confronted Trump about his habit of flagrant lying, Trump justified his behavior by claiming, "I don't want to play that game at all," but that he was forced to because the Clintons "were very nasty" and "as long as they do that, you know, I will play at whatever level I have to play at."

As with most things Trump says, this is a self-serving lie. There is no evidence that the Clintons spread fake stories about Trump in order to discredit him. On the contrary—Clinton was extremely, perhaps overly careful not to overstate her concerns about the involvement of Trump campaign officials with Russian agents who she had very good reasons to believe were trying to hack the email accounts of hundreds of people involved in her campaign.

Trump's love of conspiracy theories has endeared him to troll nation, which was ecstatic to finally have a leader who is as contemptuous of empirical truth as they are.

The Republican National Convention in particular doubled as a coming out party for the conspiracy theory crowd. Typically, the convention is dominated by the usual conservative think tanks and interest groups, who might be kooky but rarely get into the truly unhinged territory. But in 2016, the dominant presence at the convention was Infowars, a conspiracy theory website run by longtime crank Alex Jones. Reporters, including myself, were amazed. Everywhere you turned, there were people sporting Infowars gear. No one single organization had anything close to the same presence.

It was about more than T-shirts, though. It quickly became obvious that the main priority of Jones and the Infowars team was to promote the idea that Hillary Clinton was a criminal who had been getting away for far too long with her nefarious conspiracies. In this mission, they were 100 percent successful. Multiple speakers at the convention, including New Jersey governor Chris Christie, insinuated or outright claimed that Clinton had committed very serious crimes and was somehow using deceitful means to escape justice. By the end of the convention, the most popular chant, by leaps and bounds, was, "Lock her up! Lock her up!"

It's worth remembering, again, that Hillary Clinton has been subject to endless federal investigations for decades, and no one has ever found a single reason to prosecute her for anything. Meanwhile, while the crowd was chanting "lock her up," Trump's campaign was forging relationships with Russian agents and Trump was continuing to refuse to release his tax returns—which he still hasn't done, to this day.

It's not a coincidence that the right wing interest in conspiracy theories escalated at the same time that they embraced someone as corrupt as Trump to be their leader. It's yet another sign of how central the psychological concept of projection is to understanding the social dynamics of conspiracy theories. So much of what drives people to embrace conspiracy theories is a need to deflect their guilt onto others. They accuse others of what troubles their own consciences, and hope that either distracts from their own sins, or that it creates a narrative about how "everybody does it," thereby making their own misdeeds seem less bad by comparison.

Pizzagate was an intriguing example of this. The conspiracy theory started in the trolliest corners of the internet, with a group of white supremacists and self-proclaimed "men's rights activists," mainly men who are *very* interested in perpetuating the myth that domestic violence and rape are something women make up to dominate and control men.

Right off the bat, these people—almost all men—were behaving in exactly the way they are constantly accusing women of behaving. They claim that women make up fake stories of rape and sexual abuse, and that feminists are being hysterical when they argue that we live in a patriarchal society where powerful social forces shield abusers from consequences. (The feminist claim was neatly proved by the revelations about Bill Cosby, Harvey Weinstein, Donald Trump, and countless others in recent months.) And then these same anti-feminists turned around and made up a fake story of rape and sexual abuse, and claimed that the powerful social force of liberalism was shielding abusers from consequence.

The timing of Pizzagate is also quite telling. On October 8, 2016, the tape of Trump on a hot mic bragging about how he forces himself on unwilling women was released. Over the next couple of weeks, a steady trickle of stories came out of women stepping forward to attest that Trump had treated them exactly as he described on the tape. A woman stepped forward to say he groped her on a plane in 1980. A makeup artist said he repeatedly groped her in 1992. Another said he put his hand on her crotch in the early '90s. Multiple beauty pageant contestants said he would hang out and ogle them while they were naked backstage—something Trump bragged about on Howard Stern's show, as well.

"No men are anywhere, and I'm allowed to go in, because I'm the owner of the pageant and therefore I'm inspecting it," he told Stern. "You know, they're standing there with no clothes. 'Is everybody OK?' And you see these incredible-looking women, and so I sort of get away with things like that."

But despite the fact that he was on tape bragging about how much he enjoys getting away with sexual abuse and harassment, the campaign accused all of these women of lying.

After nearly three weeks of bad press about Trump, all of a sudden the right wing internet was ablaze with accusations that there was a "pedophila ring" at Comet Ping Pong, that the Clinton

Foundation was a front for it, and that it was all proved true by emails stolen from Podesta and leaked on Wikileaks. The conspiracy theorists got there by literally arguing that emails about Podesta eating pizza were somehow code for child sex trafficking.

It doesn't take a doctorate in psychology to figure out what's going on here. By inventing a fake pedophilia ring, right wing trolls were able to accomplish two goals: One, make Trump's real life transgressions seem mild by comparison—what's a little pussy-grabbing, compared to running a child sex ring? Two, disinformation campaigns work by devaluing the truth. Flooding the market with fake stories about sexual abuse teaches people to treat stories about sexual abuse with heightened levels of skepticism. If the discourse is full of people trading accusations of sexual abuse and many of them, like Pizzagate, are obviously nonsense, many people will decide it's simply easier to distrust all stories about sexual abuse—which clearly benefits men like Trump, who are almost certainly guilty. You know, due to the repeated bragging on tape and whatnot.

For many of the men spreading Pizzagate, there was also a clear personal incentive. One of the biggest social media vectors for the conspiracy theory was a man named Mike Cernovich. Cernovich used to be your standard issue grifter, a "men's rights activist" who lives off his handsome divorce settlement from his wealthy ex-wife and who self-publishes self-help books with titles like *Gorilla Mindset: How to Control Your Thoughts and Emotions and Live Life on Your Terms*, which mostly equate being a sociopathic asshole with being successful.

(Grifters love Trump, because, with his fake university and business built more on branding opportunities than actual creation, he is really the platonic idea of a successful con man.)

Cernovich also has quite the troubling history when it comes to the topic of sexual violence. In 2003, he was arrested for rape. He was able to get the charge reduced to misdemeanor battery and eventually expunged from his record after doing community service. Despite this brush with the law, Cernovich has a habit of shamelessly trolling feminists—or really anyone who thinks rape is a serious problem. He obsessively blogged about his belief that false rape accusations are more common than legal experts think and offered "advice" to readers on how to avoid those supposedly false charges.

"It's also anti-rape game," he wrote in a typical tweet on the subject. "After abusing a girl, I always immediately send a text and save her reply."

"The hotter the sex, the more closely it resembles rape," read another.

"Have you guys ever tried 'raping' a girl without using force? Try it," he whined in another tweet. "It's basically impossible. Date rape does not exist."

Despite his supposed concern about "false" rape allegations, Cernovich was eager to rush in and spread a genuinely—and *obviously*—false rape accusation against completely innocent people.

"There was a map to probably, probably child trafficking or something like that, probably the sex cult shit. That's why it was coded," he said in a video on the subject of Pizzagate.

"These people are fucking sick, man," said this man who literally complained online that women make it too hard to rape them.

Cernovich's behavior nicely illustrates why the trolling impulse is so easily married to conspiracy theory–mongering. Who knows if Cernovich really believes his own bullshit about child sex rings? What is clear, however, is that he enjoys play-acting the role of someone who is outraged over sexual abuse. Doing so allows him to simultaneously damage his political opponents while also perpetuating the idea that the only reason people make such accusations is to score political points. Cernovich clearly has a strong interest in convincing people to see sexual abuse not as a serious issue, but just as a political game played by bad faith actors.

Of course, there's often some deeper psychology at work with the projection that so many conspiracy theorists engage in. While members of troll nation often love to think of themselves in villainous terms—bragging about violence, dressing tough, displaying their willingness to be cruel like a badge of honor—most still crave the opportunity to feel like the good guy at times. Conspiracy theories allow the bad guys to play at being the good guys. It allows people who spend their time trying to dismantle progress and uphold oppression to feel like self-righteous crusaders for justice. And, because their crusades are fake, they get to have that feeling without actually doing any real good in the world or undermining the larger, more nihilistic goals of the right in the Trump era.

With the conspiracy theory mentality ensconced in the White House, it was inevitable that many in the right wing media ecosystem would feel newly emboldened to start experimenting with the joys of just making shit up. Which is how one of the dumber Clinton conspiracy theories banging around out there managed, in the Trump era, to end up on Fox News.

To be certain, Fox News has frequently played a little loose with the truth. But until recently, their particular flavor of propaganda was a lot subtler than the fake news and conspiracy-mongering that festers in some corners of the internet. Fox News often relies more on lies of omission, such as failing to cover stories that are a big deal that are unflattering to Republicans, coupled with a tendency to exaggerate the importance of things like the Benghazi investigation. Sometimes conspiracy theories were hinted at—Trump spent some time on Fox News asking "questions" about Obama's birth certificate—but really the network's strategy had mostly been to mislead viewers by distorting reality, instead of wallowing in tinfoil land, à la Alex Jones. When Glenn Beck started wandering too far off into the conspiracy theories, he was summarily fired and ended up having to create a sad little shadow empire at TheBlaze.

But Sean Hannity, a Fox News mainstay since 1996, made a bold attempt in 2017 to change all that, by getting his show deeply involved in a conspiracy theory accusing Hillary Clinton of killing a Democratic National Committee staffer named Seth Rich. The whole debacle wasn't just an assault on truth. It was a vile assault on basic human decency. And yet, in another sign of the moral rot that has eaten away at the American right, Hannity hasn't really paid a price for the role he played in tormenting the family of a murder victim.

Rich died in the early hours of the morning on July 10, 2016, a couple of weeks before a set of emails—which we now know were stolen by the Russian government—from DNC staffers were leaked on the internet through WikiLeaks. At the time of his murder, Rich was providing tech support for the DNC. The 27-year-old had gone out drinking at a favorite bar in his Washington, D.C., neighborhood, and was murdered in an apparent robbery gone wrong while out in the street a block from his home in the wee hours of the morning.

Right wing conspiracy theorists, aided by some left wing sorts who hate the Clintons, reacted to this tragedy by trying to argue that Rich—and not the Russian government—was the source who leaked the emails to WikiLeaks, and that he was murdered for it.

On its surface, the argument doesn't make sense. Conspiracy theorists want you to believe that Rich was a whistleblower trying to shine light on the DNC's efforts to "rig" the primary so Clinton beat Bernie Sanders, but there was no evidence to support this "rigging" accusation in the emails that were leaked. WikiLeaks *wanted* people to believe that—and sadly, many Sanders supporters were suckered by the accusations—but a close examination of the emails found, at best, that some people in the DNC were grumpy that Sanders wouldn't concede the race after Clinton had racked up a vote count sufficient to secure the nomination. It doesn't make sense that a whistleblower would leak something that isn't evidence. And even if it was evidence, then such a person would probably prefer leaking it to a major newspaper rather than a shady operation like WikiLeaks.

But a whole bunch of people are deeply invested in denying that the Russian government is behind the hacked emails. That group includes Julian Assange, the head of WikiLeaks, who went on Twitter to insinuate that Rich was the leaker, even though it's damn near 100 percent certain he was not. (And if Rich was the leaker, Assange could prove it. His failure to do so, even after Rich was murdered, is just one more piece of evidence that this is a disgusting exploitation of a violent crime to stoke a conspiracy theory.) That group also includes Trump supporters and the portion of Sanders supporters who got taken in by Russian propaganda and don't want to admit to themselves or others that they were fooled.

The Seth Rich conspiracy theory is an Alex Jones–level pile of bullshit, but it got a lift in mainstream media when Hannity started using his Fox News show, one of the most popular cable news shows in the country, to start selling this nonsense to his gullible audience.

Hannity had hinted at the Seth Rich conspiracy theory multiple times in the months since the young man was murdered, but in May 2017, he went all in. That's when Fox News reported that a private investigator named Rod Wheeler allegedly claimed that Seth Rich had been communicating with WikiLeaks before his death. This was untrue. The reports that Wheeler had been hired by the Rich family were false—he had been hired by a wealthy Trump supporter. The family put out a press statement flatly denying Wheeler's claims and then Wheeler himself sued the network, saying Fox News had fabricated some of his statements.

No matter. Hannity had picked up the stick and was running with it. On his Fox News show, his radio show, and Twitter account, Hannity relentlessly promoted this conspiracy theory, and one of Trump's own lawyers, Jay Sekulow, even joined in on one segment on Fox News.

Hannity's purpose was obvious: If he could convince his audience that Rich had leaked the DNC emails to WikiLeaks, then they had an excuse to dismiss the reams of real world evidence that show that hackers paid by the Russian government did it. Hannity didn't even try to hide that this was his purpose.

"Explosive developments in the mysterious murder of former DNC staffer Seth Rich that could completely shatter the narrative that in fact WikiLeaks was working with the Russians, or there was collusion between the Trump campaign and the Russians," he breathlessly declared on Fox News on May 16.

The timing of this is important to understand Hannity's desperation. On May 9, Trump had fired FBI director James Comey in an obvious bid to derail the Russia investigation. On May 11,

Trump admitted to NBC news anchor Lester Holt that his purpose was obstruction of justice, saying, "when I decided to just do it, I said to myself, I said, 'You know, this Russia thing with Trump and Russia is a made-up story.'" On May 17, Robert Mueller was appointed special counsel to investigate any potential collusion between the Trump campaign and the Russian government to commit illegal acts, such as stealing email, in order to tip the election.

(As of this writing, Mueller has secured two guilty pleas and two indictments of Trump campaign staff.)

The Rich gambit was a pathetic ploy by Hannity to tap into the conspiracy theory–minded nature of 21st century conservative America, in an effort to poison his audience against accepting any forthcoming revelations about the Trump administration's involvement with the Russian conspiracy to manipulate the American election. But it was so over the top that even Fox News turned on Hannity. On May 23, Hannity reluctantly agreed to stop embarrassing the network by flogging this story, but he still kept at it on his radio show and Twitter.

It turned out there was, in fact a conspiracy—but not among Democrats to kill Seth Rich. Instead, it was reported in August that Ed Butowsky, the wealthy Trump supporter backing Wheeler, had been in contact both with the White House and Fox News about his efforts to claim the DNC and Clinton had Rich murdered.

These sorts of political games have very real costs, and not just on election outcomes. The Rich family has suffered greatly because of the exploitation of Seth Rich's murder.

"Every day we wake up to new headlines, new lies, new factual errors, new people approaching us to take advantage of us and Seth's legacy," Mary and Joel Rich, Seth's parents, wrote in the

Washington Post on May 23. "It just won't stop. The amount of pain and anguish this has caused us is unbearable. With every conspiratorial flare-up, we are forced to relive Seth's murder and a small piece of us dies as more of Seth's memory is torn away from us."

Few things demonstrate the moral depravity and nihilism that has swept over 21st century conservative America more than the widespread embrace of conspiracy theories such as birtherism and Pizzagate. The proliferation of lies is rapidly degrading public discourse, which is why "lol nothing matters" has become the dark internet joke of our time. Worse, as the story of Seth Rich and his family shows, real people are being hurt by the rapidly growing pile of bullshit. Unfortunately, there's no real remorse from troll nation, which means we can only expect this problem to expand until it engulfs us all.

Case Study: Neil Gorsuch

Many in the mainstream media were desperate to think the best of Neil Gorsuch, Trump's first nominee to sit on the Supreme Court. So desperate, in fact, that most coverage glossed over the fact that Gorsuch had no business being appointed in the first place.

The seat in question had been open more than a year by the time Gorsuch had his confirmation hearing. In February 2016, Obama swiftly nominated a judge to fill the seat left when Justice Antonin Scalia died on a hunting trip in West Texas. Rather than do his constitutional duty and give Obama's pick, Merrick Garland, his confirmation hearing, Senate Majority Leader Mitch McConnell largely ignored Obama's nomination. The media, occupied by the Donald Trump Monkey Show that the campaign had descended into, barely noticed. And so it was, when Trump became president, McConnell could simply pretend that Obama's nomination never happened.

Rather than raise a hue and cry when McConnell flouted the constitution, giving a seat illegally to a Republican appointee without giving the Democratic appointee a fair hearing, the mainstream journalists—perhaps embarrassed at how they had utterly failed to hold McConnell accountable for his unlawful actions the year before—simply acted as if all this was normal. And, eager to believe that Trump was somehow going to be a real president instead of some clown honking out racist nonsense on Twitter, they eagerly rushed forward to declare that Gorsuch was a respectable and downright normal pick. He even looked the part, being a handsome and distinguished man with white-gray hair and high cheekbones. Surely he could not be a member of troll nation, right?

"Selecting this guy, who's clearly qualified, meets those credentials," said David Chalian of CNN, after Trump announced the pick. "Hard to really call him outside of the mainstream of judges."

"This is not somebody, as you all have pointed out, who is outside of the judicial mainstream or the establishment mainstream, I should say," said Kasie Hunt of MSNBC.

"It seems like the choice of Judge Gorsuch is a relatively mainstream choice that you might expect from any Republican president," said even Rachel Maddow, the liberal lion of MSNBC.

Insofar that Gorsuch is "mainstream," it just shows that the mainstream right had become inseparable from its trollier faction. Because, it turned out, Gorsuch is a first class troll. It's not just that he's a hardline right-winger, though he is definitely that. It's also that he's such an obnoxious prick that even many conservatives find him repulsive. And these people think Rush Limbaugh is an acceptable dinner guest.

"Part of the reason I'm fascinated by Neil Gorsuch is I can't believe he's a real person," noted Ian Millhiser, the justice editor at ThinkProgress, on Twitter. "He's the guy from a '80s college comedy who leads the rich kids frat and winds up with a pile of garbage dumped on him in the movie's penultimate scene."

Millhiser is joking, but barely. It was revealed during the confirmation hearings that Gorsuch spent his high school and college years as that pompous know-it-all twit whose only mode is condescending to all the human beings he thinks are beneath him.

He was also a troll. He started a "Fascism Forever" club at Georgetown Preparatory School in the '80s, which was allegedly a joke to tweak the noses of liberals. (That's, of course, what all trolls say when the actual content of their arguments is indefensible.) And, like every other troll who hides behind "free speech," Gorsuch, who went to college at Columbia University, argued that barring military recruiters from campus due to the '80s era ban on gay service members was somehow a violation of the "inalienable right to express himself or herself."

(Needless to say, the idea that military recruiters are freely expressing their own opinions, rather than saying what the military wants them to, is laughable beyond belief. If any of these recruiters dared criticize military polices, it's doubtful that Gorsuch would argue that they had a free speech right to defy their employer.)

But while he believed in the "free speech" of military recruiters to say exactly what the military wants them to, when it came to actual students freely expressing their actual opinions, Gorsuch wasn't such a fan.

"Our protestors, it seems, have a monopoly on righteousness," he sneered in a piece denouncing protesters for defending a woman from being evicted from her university-owned apartment. "In all their muddled thinking, however, our 'progressives' have become anything but truly progressive."

Speech gets freer, in true troll fashion, the closer it gets to the authoritarian way of thinking.

What swiftly became clear after Gorsuch got to the court—but should have been clear long before he got there—is that while his hair is gray now, he is still that asshole.

In October, NPR's Nina Totenberg, perhaps the best-sourced journalist covering the Supreme Court in the country, came forward with a genuinely startling revelation: Gorsuch was alienating his colleagues on the court. Gorsuch "ticks off some members of the court—and I don't think it's just the liberals," she said on her podcast, adding that Justice Elena Kagan in particular has been butting heads with Gorsuch in conference, which are the judges-only meetings the court has to settle decisions.

"Gorsuch, who was confirmed last spring and this week began his first full term, has shaken relations at the high court with actions that show—depending on one's view—a degree of arrogance or independence," reported Joan Biskupic of CNN, adding that there was so much "ill will" that there's a very real danger that some of the more conservative judges will be tempted to shift left on certain issues, rather than agree with a chucklehead like Gorsuch. Scalia, she noted, likely pushed Justice Sandra Day O'Connor to the left by being so condescending to her at times, and Gorsuch reportedly talks like that to everyone.

Gorsuch, operating on the premise that he's too good to mix it up with such mortals as the senior justices, skipped the first justices-only meeting after his confirmation. He interrupts other justices frequently and talks down to everyone during the really time-limited oral arguments for cases, in between bouts of lecturing the court audience about his tedious and frankly silly ideas on the Constitution.

It's hard to overstate how odd Gorsuch's behavior is. The Supreme Court has, until now, largely been a place of congenial relationships, even between people who have wildly different political views. The bad blood between Scalia and O'Connor was unusual, and Gorsuch has gone beyond that, seeming indifferent to what bridges he burns with his colleagues.

Gorsuch's belief that he is not bound by the same rules and traditions as other people came out in his decisions. One particularly noteworthy dissent was his opinion on a case regarding the birth certificates of children born to couples in same-sex marriages. In the decision that legalized same-sex marriage, *Obergefell v. Hodges*, Justice Anthony Kennedy *explicitly* noted that one of the benefits of marriage was the right of spouses to have their names on birth and death certificates. Even Justice John Roberts, no fan of same-sex marriage, agreed in this case that Obergefell's precedent should guarantee the right of same-sex couples to both be named as parents on a birth certificate.

But not Gorsuch, whose self-regarded intellectual prowess is not bound by earthly concerns, such as what the law actually says. Nor, apparently is he bound by anything as boring as facts. As Mark Joseph Stern at *Slate* pointed out, Gorsuch flatly misstated the facts of the case in his dissent, completely stating in his opinion that the Arkansas law already granted same-sex couples this right, when the whole point of the suit was that it did not.

When confronted with the fact that Gorsuch said something flat-out false in his dissent, his office told Stern, "the Court does not comment on its opinions, which speak for themselves."

Trump *could* have appointed a more traditional conservative, like Roberts. It wouldn't have really made that much of a difference, in terms of court decisions. Traditional conservatives oppose liberal criminal justice laws, voting rights, abortion rights, LGBT rights, and would likely even give Trump wide berth to use his executive powers to shield himself from the legal consequences of whatever the hell is going on with him and Russia.

But, no, in the era of troll nation, it's not enough to appoint someone who simply is terrible on all matters of policy. He also has to thumb his nose at the rule of law and basic good manners. Gorsuch has a lifetime appointment to the highest court in the land because it wasn't enough to just anger liberals. No, their noses had to be rubbed in the loss of a seat that, by all rights, was Obama's to fill. Trump had a slate of potential nominees to pick from. The fact that he landed on one of the biggest assholes to ever take up residence in Washington, D.C., cannot be a coincidence.

Chapter 9

The Media

One of the distinguishing traits of the troll-style politics that dominates Trump-era conservatism is the utter disregard for any values outside of winning at all costs and, perhaps even more importantly, defeating liberals. Decency, political norms, and truth itself are all treated as acceptable casualties in the endless quest to fuck with the left.

But while many of the excesses of the right seem new, the reality is that the Trumpian right is just the outgrowth from roots laid years, even decades ago, in the American right. The racism and sexism, the conspiracy theories, the harping about political correctness? All of it goes back decades, and is only exploding out of control now because the right wing political infrastructure has let these foul ideologies and stupid ideas flourish for so long.

Nowhere is this more obvious than when it comes to Trump's war on the media. All his lies and outrageous accusations can be traced directly back to decades of right wing pundits and politicians encouraging conservative voters to believe that mainstream media sources have a "liberal bias" and are not to be trusted. Trump simply takes it to the next level, dispensing with the notion that truth and facts themselves are relevant and insisting that the validity of a news report depends entirely on how flattering he finds it.

"Fake news" started as a banal term, invented by Buzzfeed reporters, to describe fabricated stories that were being passed off by hoaxsters as real news reports. Soon, however, Trump, whose ego was bruised by hearing that fake news had helped elect him, started aggressively using the term "fake news" to demonize any news he disapproves of. Soon, the usage was picked up across the right, and now the term is almost exclusively used to mean news that is actually true, but conservatives reject for ideological reasons.

It's particularly disconcerting to witness the way conservatives yell "fake news" at every unfavorable news story with an unmitigated glee. They know that cavalierly dismissing obviously factual stories as "fake" really aggravates liberals, and trolling the left is for right-wingers, circa 2018, an activity more pleasurable than sex.

Calling obviously true news "fake news" is gaslighting, a form of manipulation where the manipulator tells blatant lies to the victim and, when called out, stands by the lies, often blaming the target's supposed mental damage if the target insists that the truth is true.

Gaslighting people, especially women, by calling them "crazy" for rejecting his lies is a favorite practice of Trump's. He's questioned the sanity of Mika Brzezinski, Megyn Kelly, Maureen

Dowd, and Bernie Sanders, among others, for the high crime of saying things about him that happened to be true.

"In authoritarian governments," Brian Klaas writes in *The Despot's Apprentice*, gaslighting "aims to force citizens to question their own sanity, rather than the government's narrative. Winston's experience in *1984* was an example of systematic gaslighting."

Most authoritarian governments go about gaslighting with the utmost seriousness, using the power of the state and social pressure to get citizens to agree, like Winston in *1984*, that 2+2=5. The "fake news" gambit, however, is something different and possibly new. Rather than trying to induce insanity by making liberals question reality itself, conservatives are trying to *make* liberals go crazy by trolling them. All conservatives need to do is keep a straight face while insisting that they believe that 2+2=5, and liberals will exhaust all their mental and emotional reserves trying to explain that no, really, 2+2=4. Eventually, conservatives will point to the frazzled, distraught state of liberals begging people to believe that 2+2=4 and laugh and say, "What a nutjob!"

What are conservatives thinking when they call something "fake news"? What is Trump thinking? It's hard to imagine conservatives *literally* believe that the media is making stories up about the Trump-Russia investigation or that Trump had smaller inauguration crowds than Obama. Instead, the Republican war on media needs to be understood more as a rejection of truth as a value. To call something "fake news" isn't to say that it's real or not real, but a way of indicating that truth itself doesn't matter— that the only thing that matters is loyalty to Trump and the right wing tribe. Telling lies, in fact, is recast as a fun, sporting way to annoy liberals, and to punish liberals for their goody-two-shoes politically correct insistence that facts matter.

Dan Kahan, a Yale professor of law and psychology, runs the Cultural Cognition Project, a research project dedicated to studying how things like identity and social values shape people's understanding of facts. When I interviewed him in 2016 about the tendency of Trump supporters to proudly declare their allegiance to false, often plainly ridiculous beliefs, he explained that, for many conservatives, saying these kinds of things is a "kind of middle finger" to liberals, and less an expression of their real world understanding of empirical fact.

For instance, a 2014 study published in Public Opinion Quarterly found that a conservative's answer to questions about Obama's birthplace was heavily shaped by what he thought the purpose of the question was. If the researchers presented the question as a quiz about how knowledgeable the subjects were of political facts, and the subjects felt they were being judged based on the accuracy of the answers, conservatives were more likely to give the correct answer (Hawaii). But when, the researchers wrote, the question was framed in political terms, more conservatives saw it as "an opportunity to express anti-Obama sentiment by challenging the legitimacy of his presidency."

Claiming Obama was born in Kenya isn't experienced by a lot of conservatives as a direct statement of belief about the material facts. It's that espousing birtherism satisfies the emotional desire to undermine a black man's legitimate claim to the Oval Office, without having to come out and plainly state that the birther doesn't believe black people should be eligible to hold office.

"People have a stake in some position being true," Kahan told me, "because the status of their group or their standing in it depends on that answer."

"Part of the reason they might be doing it is because they know it's really going to get an aversive response from people who have an alternative identity and who know that's the true answer," he added.

In other words, they're trolling.

Everyone does this, it must be said, to some degree. We all, liberal or conservative, sometimes say things because that's what's expected of us and not because it's what we really think or believe. But the gap between left and right has widened dramatically in recent years, to the point where conservatives, particularly Trump loyalists, flatly reject the idea that truth even matters.

"If Jesus Christ gets down off the cross and told me Trump is with Russia," one Trump supporter told CNN a year after the election, "I would tell him, 'Hold on a second. I need to check with the President if it's true.'"

Of course, your average secularist liberal might quibble with the idea that Jesus Christ has some special access to the empirical truth, but let's just glide past that to look at what this man's metaphor is conveying: He's basically admitting that he values Trump's instructions on what to believe over what *a god who is forbidden to lie* is telling him. His expression is a fanciful way of saying that he simply doesn't care what is true. All he cares about is believing what Trump tells him to believe.

Reading the quote on the page is one thing, but watching the video really shows how clever this man thought this line was. It felt like a practiced line, a joke he trotted out for the knowing chuckles of his fellow Trump lovers. The anchor who asked the question hadn't even *mentioned* Russia, but the Trump supporter just knew he had this killer line and goddammit, he was going to say it on live TV. It worked as hoped on his fellow panelists, most of whom smiled in shared satisfaction.

And why shouldn't they? Liberals were bound to hear that line and go absolutely bonkers. Every time a liberal works himself into an outrage, right-wingers count that as a win, even if the cost of provoking that reaction is playing a chucklehead on national television.

Against this backdrop, mainstream media doesn't even have a chance. Journalists can carefully double check all their facts and gather multiple reliable sources for any report, but if the story is ideologically inconvenient for conservatives, it will be dismissed as "fake news." Truth is something those liberals care about, and refusing to care about anything liberals care about is a point of pride for troll nation.

The utter shamelessness of conservatives on this front can be breathtaking, but this contempt for truth was not a trait that was formed overnight. Instead, it took years of careful propaganda, geared at provoking conservative insecurities and resentments, to get right-wingers to the point where they care less about facts than they care about sticking it to those liberals.

Complaints about mainstream media bias against conservatives have been aired on the right for decades. Historian Nicole Hemmer traced the narrative back to the 1940s, when a nascent conservative media emerged in publishing and radio, fueled by arguments that it was necessary to have this right wing media to balance against a mainstream media hopelessly distorted by liberal bias.

In the 1960s, Hemmer argued in the *Atlantic*, conservatives decided, in addition to having a media of their own, they "would also have to discredit existing media."

At stake was the Fairness Doctrine, which the FCC adopted in 1949 to encourage political debate on TV and radio. The rule was fairly straightforward: If a show or station had a conservative viewpoint, equal time was to be offered to a liberal viewpoint. (Or vice versa.) But, as Hemmer explained, conservatives "viewed objectivity as a mask concealing entrenched liberal bias, hiding the slanted reporting that dominated American media. Because of this, the right believed fairness did not require a response to conservative broadcasts; conservative broadcasts were the response."

This belief, that any view not explicitly conservative must be liberal, has become the first station of the right wing cross of victimhood. Mainstream media sources have, in the decades since, bent over backwards to assure conservative audiences that it isn't true, to no avail.

Trying to convince the right that mainstream media isn't biased towards the left has often reached levels of absurdity. The *New York Times* repeatedly fell into this trap during the 2016 campaign, running stories on Hillary Clinton that were poorly sourced, speculative, or based on rumor—usually pitched to them by right wing sources. Shoddy stories about her health, her emails, and the Clinton Foundation that would have never passed the pitch meeting if they were about a Republican instead of a Democratic candidate routinely made it to the front page of the *New York Times*.

It's likely not because the newspaper is secretly conservative, but because the *New York Times* editors are so overeager to disprove accusations of liberal bias that they give conservative-friendly stories a handicap that would never be given to any other kind of story.

Fox News, still the country's most popular propaganda outlet, built its entire brand on this notion that any media that doesn't have an explicitly conservative viewpoint is inherently liberal. The network's motto for decades, "fair and balanced," intrinsically accused other media sources of being anything but fair and balanced.

It was a nifty little trick. A motto like that not only demonizes more even-handed media sources, but it implies that there's something more trustworthy about the information Fox News is handing out. Repeated studies, however, show that Fox News viewers are less informed about the news than other news consumers. A 2016 study from Fairleigh Dickinson University actually demonstrated that people who took in *no news at all* were better informed about current events than Fox News viewers. (NPR listeners were the best informed.)

Fox News works primarily as a propaganda outlet whose viewers have an almost cult-like loyalty. Anyone who has conservative friends or relatives over the age of 50 has probably witnessed the way that Fox News has become the wallpaper of red state life, turned on all day to pipe out a steady stream of balderdash. The ratings bear this impression out. For 16 years now, Fox News has been the number one cable news network.

But Fox News does more than indoctrinate elderly white people day in and out. Even though it's dropped it's provocative "fair and balanced" slogan, the existence of the channel helps feed this narrative that all other media is hopelessly biased towards the left. That narrative, in turn, is used to guilt-trip mainstream media into publishing or broadcasting conservative misinformation in a fruitless bid to seem more fair and balanced themselves.

The recent hire of Bret Stephens at the *New York Times* exposes this problem. Stephens is a climate change denialist. Granted, he's one of the more genteel climate change denialists, the ones who present themselves as having "doubts" rather than raving about the international communist conspiracy to foist this global warming hoax. But honestly, it should be no matter. As a journalistic institution, the *New York Times* had a responsibility not to hire someone who refuses to adhere to the baseline norm of accepting empirical reality that all journalists should be held to. But the relentless accusations of "liberal bias" clearly got to the leadership at the *New York Times*, and in order to show off their supposed objectivity, they hired someone who literally objects to objective reality. No liberal journalist who believed, for instance, that 9/11 was an inside job would get a similar position. But fear of "bias" accusations caused the *New York Times* to lower its standards to let a right wing conspiracy theorist onto its pages.

There's now an entire cottage industry of conservative hoaxsters exploiting the journalist fear of being accused of liberal bias to plant false stories in the mainstream news cycle. These hoaxsters realize that journalists are so afraid of the accusation that they will lower their evidence standards significantly and run with stories that, if they were offered by anyone other than conservative activists, would tickle journalist skepticism. The fear of being called "biased" has caused many unfortunate incidents of journalists abandoning due diligence.

I myself felt this pressure in 2015, when a group calling itself the Center for Medical Progress released a series of videos it claimed proved that Planned Parenthood clinics were selling fetal tissue for a profit. I was writing for a women's blog at the time, and my editor reached out and asked me to write about it.

I had been covering the reproductive rights issue, as a blogger then as a journalist, for almost a decade and so I strongly suspected that an anti-choice activist named Lila Rose, who works closely with right wing hoaxsters like James O'Keefe, had a hand in this. She had, with her group Live Action, been making hoax videos for years that used creative editing to try to frame Planned Parenthood, as O'Keefe had framed ACORN, as a group that was somehow involved in prostitution. But her efforts were weak sauce, and mainstream journalists had caught on to her inherent dishonesty, making her name and her organization's brand toxic. I told my editor that I thought this new organization was likely invented to circumvent the toxicity that had developed around Rose's brand.

Luckily for me, I was blessed with editors who heard my concerns about elevating a story I had very good reason to fear was a right wing hoax, and were willing to give me the time to do research to learn more before I wrote.

My suspicions only rose when Mollie Hemingway at the Federalist, a right wing site, wrote an article accusing the mainstream media of a "blackout" on the Planned Parenthood story a mere *six hours* after the first edited video was posted. First of all, most news outlets don't exactly follow what right wing cranks are chattering about on their blogs minute by minute, so even though the video was technically published at 8 AM, the first anyone who isn't a rabid religious right-winger had heard of it was hours later. Second of all, even if a journalist had seen the video the second it was punished, six hours was not enough time to do necessary fact-checking on the frankly preposterous (and later proven false) accusations made in the video.

It was clear to me that conservatives were turning up the pressure on mainstream media to publish stories on these accusations without taking the time to do basic things like research to find out if there was any credibility to them.

There could only be one reason to be exerting so much pressure on journalists to run a story without doing even the bare minimum of research: fear that such research would prove that the videos were a hoax and blow the lid off the whole thing.

Again, luckily for me, my editors got this. So while my blog post on this perhaps came out an hour or two—heaven forbid!—after many other outlets got their headlines out, I was proud of the work we did focusing on the very strong likelihood that this was a hoax. Which turned out, of course, to be true. Later, more in-depth reporting from mainstream outlets revealed that Planned Parenthood does not sell fetal tissue, and instead they facilitate donations made by the abortion patients themselves. In addition, the tissue donation is far more "pro-life" than anything anti-choice activists ever do, because it's used for research that helps save lives.

The whole thing gave me an up-close view of how conservatives leverage the accusation of "liberal bias" to get favorable coverage that is insufficiently skeptical of outlandish right wing claims. False accusations of bias were heavily, and in some cases effectively, applied to get news outlets to run overly credulous stories about the accusations in these videos.

Eventually, most reputable news organizations did do follow-up stories verifying that the accusations were false and the whole thing was a hoax, but it was too late. The stories reporting that accusations were made but didn't clarify that the accusations were false were already out there. And to this day, the lie that Planned Parenthood sells "baby parts" is a widespread belief on the right.

This little bit of media manipulation eventually led to murder. On November 27, 2015, a man named Robert Dear walked into the Planned Parenthood in Colorado Springs, Colorado, and opened fire on the clinic. Three people were killed and nine people were injured. After Dear was arrested, he gave a rambling interview where he said, "No more baby parts." So far, none of the people involved in the hoax videos have expressed remorse about inspiring this deadly act of terrorism.

In general, there's a disturbing lack of moral accountability on the right for the results of their multi-decade war on not just the free press, but the very notion of truth itself. Even after decades of sowing distrust of the media led directly to the election of a shameless liar like Trump, most conservative pundits are uninterested in grappling with the consequences of the Republican war on the media.

Trump wasn't in office a month before he went full dictator in his rhetoric about the press, declaring on Twitter, "The FAKE NEWS media (failing @nytimes, @NBCNews, @ABC, @CBS, @CNN) is not my enemy, it is the enemy of the American People!"

Trump also has a habit of characterizing the media as the "opposition party," language he appears to have picked up from Breitbart. He has also made threats. He tweeted in October 2017, "With all of the Fake News coming out of NBC and the Networks, at what point is it appropriate to challenge their License?" after NBC reported an unflattering but accurate report about Trump's ignorance regarding nuclear weaponry.

The good news is that the Constitution puts some hard limits on what the government can actually do to silence the free press, though with Trump rapidly stuffing the federal judiciary with loyalists, even that right might be in more danger than many realize. But when it comes to his supporters, Trump doesn't even really need to silence the free press. Instead, he's managed to poison the well against the press so thoroughly that his supporters flatly reject true news and embrace propaganda. Even when facing seemingly undeniable facts that Trump doesn't like, Trump fans will choose loyalty to their leader over objective reality.

Political scientist Brian Schaffner and polling expert Samantha Luks proved this in the *Washington Post* shortly after the inauguration. Trump had started insisting that his inauguration crowd was bigger than Obama's had been, a claim which photographic evidence had shown to be comically false. Pictures from Trump's inauguration showed the D.C. Mall to be more than half empty, whereas the photos from Obama's inauguration showed that the Mall was completely packed and the crowd was spilling into the nearby streets.

Many Trump supporters, even after looking at the pictures, refused to accept the extremely obvious fact that Obama's inauguration was much bigger, likely more than double the size of Trump's. Forty percent of Trump voters insisted that the photo from Obama's inauguration was actually a picture of Trump's inauguration. Even more bizarrely, 15 percent of Trump voters just flat insisted that the picture that showed a more than half-empty Mall had more people in it than the picture of the packed Mall taken at Obama's inauguration. They knew the under-attended inauguration was Trump's, and rather than admit that few people could bother to show, they literally denied what their own eyeballs were telling them.

A similarly strange phenomenon is playing out with the Russia-Trump story. Even after Donald Trump Jr. *admitted* to meeting with Russian operatives promising dirt on Clinton, only 45 percent of Trump voters would agree that such a meeting had taken place. A July 2017 poll found that only 9 percent of Republican voters admit that Russia tried to influence the U.S. election, even though that's been verified by both independent analysis and U.S. intelligence services. Worse, that number was down from 18 percent of Republicans accepting the truth in April. The more facts about Russia's efforts to influence the election come out, the less Republicans are willing to believe them.

That's the logic of troll nation at work. The media is the "enemy," and so denying what the media says is paramount, no matter how true it obviously is. And the more that the media covers a true story, the more fiercely it's denied.

As noted earlier, it's quite likely many of these Republicans know that they are, on some level, saying a thing that is untrue. If hooked up to a lie detector or told they'd be fined $100 for every false thing they said, it's likely many to most of these Republicans would reconsider their beliefs regarding Russia. But absent that pressure, most of these people have been caught in this thought process: The media says Russia was trying to influence the media, Trump says the media is the enemy, therefore we cannot believe anything journalists say, no matter how obviously true it is.

To be clear, most people are capable of lying to themselves or believing false things, especially when there are strong emotional motivations in place. As a journalist who works in overtly liberal media, I constantly deal with liberal readers who get caught up in flattering conspiracy theories or fantasies. (For every true thing said about the Russia-Trump story, for instance, about three cockamamie ideas were spreading around left wing Twitter.) Even on a non-political level, we see this all the time: people who refuse to accept their partner is cheating, people who believe their perfectly average kids are geniuses, people who are convinced the referee has it out for their team in particular.

But there can be no doubt that Trump's war on the media has exploited and amplified this human tendency to cling to appealing lies. It's not just that Trump supporters are rejecting individual stories that they don't like, but they've rejected the entire idea that the press tells the truth. They've embraced an umbrella belief that the mainstream media literally makes stuff up on a daily basis in order to turn the public against Trump.

"More than three-quarters of Republican voters, 76 percent, think the news media invent stories about Trump and his administration, compared with only 11 percent who don't think so," Politico reported in October 2017. "Among Democrats, one-in-five think the media make up stories, but a 65 percent majority think they do not."

This is a conspiracy theory, of course, and like the ones discussed in the previous chapter, it's one rooted in projection. The mainstream press doesn't make stuff up, but Trump absolutely does. The *Washington Post* has been tracking Trump's lies and, as of this writing, has found that he makes an average 5.5 false claims a day. Worse, as the pressure has been mounting on Trump, he has been lying more frequently. By the time this book comes out, odds are the average number of lies per day has escalated.

To make it worse, the *Washington Post* is being rather conservative in what it counts as a lie. For instance, I would classify every accusation of "fake news" as a lie, because it's a term Trump uses almost exclusively to describe factually correct reports. The *Post* researchers likely didn't want to get into a debate over whether that's an actual claim Trump is making or just some jackass thing he says, and so let many of these instances go.

There's a sick genius to floating a theory that the media simply invents fake stories to discredit Trump. Every unflattering or politically inconvenient story that comes out just gets slotted into the existing "fake news" conspiracy theory. No mental energy needs to be expended inventing new rationalizations or excuses, by either the Trump administration or his followers. Once one accepts the premise that the media lies about Trump regularly, then nothing journalists say need be accepted.

Trump himself appears quite cognizant of how this works. In November, the *New York Times* reported that he had been privately claiming to at least one senator and one advisor that the tape of him bragging about kissing and groping women against their will was not real, even though he had admitted it was when the tape was released in October 2016.

Needless to say, Trump is lying here. It's not even the first time he has outright lied about something he did that was caught on tape. Trump has repeatedly denied that he mocked disabled journalist Serge Kovaleski, even though there's a video out there of him deriding Kovaleski while doing an impression of the physical effects of Kovaleski's disability.

Trump lies so much about what he's said in the past, on video, that the Clinton campaign was able to assemble a campaign ad showing Trump denying previously videotaped statements made about global warming, the national debt, the war on Iraq, women's rights, and what he's paid in taxes.

My take on what Trump is doing by claiming it wasn't him on the *Access Hollywood* tape is that he's beta testing his lie. He's running it past people in his own life, to see if they visibly blanch or even protest, and gauging whether or not this is a lie too big even for his loyal followers.

And why shouldn't he believe that his followers would swallow this obvious lie? They've swallowed hundreds, frankly thousands of others. His followers believe the media deliberately makes up stories to discredit Trump. So why not take that belief to the next level? Why not believe that the *Washington Post* had some Hollywood special effects geeks fake this video? The "fake news" concept that Republicans have broadly embraced really has no limit—anything could be called a fake, and no level of proof will ever be good enough.

Hating the media has an emotional component to it that is impervious to reason. The war on media has a strong culture war vibe to it, one that has been fed by right wing pundits for generations. Journalists, like academics, are stereotyped as an overeducated elite, too busy eating expensive food in designer clothes and having exotic sex on silk sheets to care about "real" America. Troll nation really wants to believe this about journalists, even though the grim reality is that the news industry is struggling and most journalists are overworked, underpaid, and struggling to keep their heads above water in the age of the internet.

The conservative commitment to this stereotype about the media "elite," coupled with unprecedented access readers have to journalists through social media, creates a bizarre daily ritual for journalists. Many journalists have social media feeds full of people with more job security and wealth accusing them, daily, of being a pampered elite that has no idea what a real day's work looks like. It's a first row look at how central the concept of trolling has become to the American right.

Shortly after Trump declared journalists "the enemy of the American People," I briefly met a prominent Democratic politician. "I just want you to know that, no matter what the president says, you are not the enemy," he told me with that corny sincerity that all politicians master and most journalists, particularly of the wears-jeans-to-work sort like myself, find kind of embarrassing. It was hard to know what to say because I had experienced Trump's Twitter whining about the media the same way I experience all Twitter whining from trolls, as ranting from a person who has made being an asshole his life's philosophy, and thus not really an argument or an idea worth engaging with.

Still, I appreciated this politician taking the time to say this, as weird as it felt in the moment, because it's easy to get lulled. Trump is a troll with the emotional maturity of a literal toddler (except toddlers have more capacity for reason and empathy). His support comes from a group of people who think "suck it, libtards" is an acceptable substitute for having ideas or political views. The whole thing is beyond absurd.

And yet, the fact that the Trump coalition has no real views beyond wanting to damage liberals doesn't mean they don't present a very serious threat. It's clear that it's led the country to this point where our free press is being regularly threatened by the president and his supporters, who have convinced themselves that responsible journalism is just one more annoying liberal affectation that needs to be destroyed. Their anger is ridiculous, but they still have the power to turn their silly bigotries into real life attacks on the journalistic institutions that protect our democracy.

Conclusion

Will There Be an End to the Trolling?

The ability of Republicans to set aside all common sense and vote for a clown like Donald Trump set the mainstream media scurrying off for answers. One cause, reasonably enough, that many journalists landed on was political polarization, which has accelerated in recent years due to tribalist self-sorting of liberals and conservatives, gerrymandering efforts orchestrated by Republicans, and a variegated media environment (including social media) that allows audiences more freedom than ever to sculpt their own media diet to their ideological liking.

One of the main reasons Hillary Clinton managed to lose the election despite getting nearly 3 million more votes than Trump is that this polarization has concentrated Democratic voters into urban areas, while Republicans dominate the suburban and rural areas that tend, due to the way the American electoral system is designed, to have representational power disproportionate to

actual population. And those Republicans have become so tribalist that it just made sense to vote for an idiot like Trump for
the sheer pleasure of offending those urban liberals they hate so
much.

"This is not about policy. The chasm between left and right
during much of the Cold War was far wider than it is today on
certain issues," Fareed Zakaria of the *Washington Post* wrote in
June 2017. "Partisanship today is more about identity."

There's certainly evidence to back up Zakaria's sense that this
divide is more a matter of culture and identity than, say, one's
view on nationalizing the auto industry or beliefs about the ideal
marginal tax rate. The polarization that shows up in polling data
shows that Republicans and Democrats are increasingly sus-
picious of and angry at each other. Fifty years ago, almost no
Americans indicated disapproval of a child marrying someone
from a different party, but now one-third of Democrats and half
of Republicans disapprove.

"More than half of Democrats (55 percent) say the Republican
Party makes them 'afraid,' while 49 percent of Republicans say
the same about the Democratic Party," Pew Research indicated in
a report released in June 2016. Of those highly engaged in politics,
"fully 70 percent of Democrats and 62 percent of Republicans say
they are afraid of the other party."

Sadly, most of the media response to this has been to declare
a pox on both houses, acting as if conservatives and liberals are
equally responsible for this growing distrust and divide—which,
in turn, implies that both sides are being irrational in their
partisanship.

"People on the other side of the divide are not just wrong and
to be argued with," Zakaria described, refusing to consider the

possibility of substantive difference between the anger of the right and the anger of the left. He piously concluded, "I, for one, will keep arguing that liberals and conservatives should open themselves to all kinds of opinions and ideas that differ from their own."

"It has become policy only to oppose and obstruct, investigate or call news conferences to demand more investigations, not propose and construct," John Zogby wrote in another self-congratulatory March 2017 opinion piece in *Forbes*. "This situation only further fuels the rage we see now coming from all sides."

It's hard not to marvel at the commitment that some pundits have to the "both sides do it equally" narrative in a year when the Democrats ran a mainstream liberal with decades of political experience under the banner of "Stronger Together," while the Republicans ran an inexperienced reality TV star who pandered to white supremacists and was caught on tape bragging about sexually assaulting women. Pretending that both sides do it equally has never been an adequate strategy to achieve much-longed-for objectivity, but lately the efforts smack of delusion.

The half of Democrats that say Republicans make them afraid, it's worth noting, gave that answer right as Republicans were *nominating Trump* to be president. Republicans, on the other hand, were flipping out about a woman who was a member of the administration of a man who'd been president and presided over a recovering economy while maintaining a corruption-free White House for 8 years. Democratic fear was a rational response to their environment. Republican fear has been constructed out of decades of well-funded right wing media demonizing liberals by portraying them as a fifth column bent on destroying America.

The evidence simply doesn't support the idea that partisan warfare is a matter of both sides acting irrationally for no reason. The evidence points to the conclusion that conservatives are the ones who escalated hostilities, and liberal anger is a legitimate response to being constantly demonized and trolled by a bunch of partisans who seek nothing but their destruction.

In March, the *Columbia Journalism Review* published a study showing that Clinton supporters during the campaign had a diverse media diet, consuming news from both left-leaning sources like MSNBC and Salon and traditional, objective media sources such as the *New York Times* and CNN. Trump supporters, however, consumed a diet that was far more tilted to right wing sites like Breitbart and Drudge. The *New York Times*, HuffPost, and the *Washington Post* were the most popular sites for Clinton supporters online. Breitbart, Fox News, and Gateway Pundit—a conspiracy theorist blogger who frequently winks at white supremacists—were the most popular sites for Trump supporters. The Hill was the only objective news source to rank in the top for Republican voters.

Even this survey underrates the scale of the problem, because when liberals do consume openly left-leaning media, it tends to be of a higher quality than the right wing media feeding conservatives. Popular left-leaning sites like Salon, Talking Points Memo, and Mother Jones have a viewpoint but they also have stronger editorial standards than sources such as Fox News and Breitbart, which have promoted hoaxes and conspiracy theories.

This divergence—where liberals get news from more objective, mainstream sources and conservatives feed primarily from conservative sources that often peddle misinformation—was a problem long before Trump got his campaign rolling. In 2014, Pew Research found similar results, with liberals turning to

CNN, PBS, and NPR, whereas conservatives loved Fox News and Rush Limbaugh.

By inoculating a belief that liberals are out to destroy America, conservatives have actually set into motion a series of events that could very well destroy America. It's not just because of Trump, either. Prior to Trump, Republican officials were swiftly moving to undermine our democratic systems, passing laws across the country designed to make it harder to vote, especially for young people and people of color, and gerrymandering districts to make already undervalued Democratic votes count for even less.

Political polarization should be understood in cause-and-effect terms, rather than just assuming everyone in the country irrationally became hyper-partisan overnight. Instead, conservatives, feeding on a well-funded right wing media for decades, became extremely hostile. Liberals, afraid and feeling under attack, grew angry in response.

Liberals are *right* to feel under attack. Right wing media demonizing liberals has led to serious consequences. Conservatives keep voting to piss off the liberals, and don't seem to care that the people they vote for wreck the environment, undermine human rights, dismantle the social safety net, start wars, and wreck the economy. Piously judging liberals for their anger, under the circumstances, verges on victim-blaming.

This is the part of the book where I'm supposed to offer solutions, perhaps a ray of hope that we can get through to troll nation, make them see the error of their ways. Unfortunately, there is no such solution. History and social science both suggest that an empowered group of authoritarians like Trump supporters will not let go of the liberal-hating mania that brought them to this point. And no matter how many times the *New York*

Times or CNN sends reporters to Trump country to ask people if they regret their choice yet, they're going to continue to get the same answer: Endless variations of, "Hell no and fuck liberals."

I want, so very badly, for these folks to be reachable. I want Trump America to wake up and say, "You know, I was foolish to be so goddamn angry because some black football players kneeled during the anthem, especially since they are right that police brutality is unacceptable." I want them to say, "It's dumb of me to keep griping about feminists wanting 'free' birth control when my spouse and I also take advantage of insurance coverage of contraception." I want them, so fucking badly, to say, "Seeing women in hijabs or hearing people speak Spanish in the supermarket doesn't affect me at all, and I vow from here on to stop being angry about something that does me, quite literally, no harm."

But, as the saying goes, you can't reason someone out of a position they didn't reason themselves into.

We can't fix troll nation. Ironically, however, accepting that we cannot fix troll nation might be the first step towards fixing America.

It gets lost in the shuffle, but I find it helpful to remind myself on a regular, ideally daily basis that Clinton got 2,868,691 more votes than Trump in 2016. Only Barack Obama, in 2008, had a higher vote count than she did. And the blunt fact of the matter is that it was only so close because so few Americans vote. According to multiple post-election analyses, including at FiveThirtyEight and the *Washington Post*, Clinton almost certainly would have won the election by a healthy electoral margin if the 42 percent of eligible voters who sat out 2016 had voted.

Conservatives have become a bitter minority of people defined primarily by white identity politics and a burning hatred of "liberals," a group that has grown to encompass most people of color, LGBT people, white people who find bigotry distasteful—basically, *everyone else.*

Trolls don't have the numbers but, as anyone who has been targeted by a troll storm online understands, their uncanny organizing skills create power far outside what their meager numbers should give them. Their hate gives them that power. It's hard to organize people behind a positive vision, because there's as many ideas about what direction the group should be headed in as there are people in the group. But flagging a target to hate—liberals, journalists, kneeling football players—creates a singular, simplistic goal that is easy to rally the haters behind.

Still, liberals should take comfort in knowing that we have the numbers, even if we have a harder time organizing. It means we don't need to convert the trolls to non-troll status to win. Like Dorothy at the end of *The Wizard of Oz*, we need to recognize that we've had the power this whole time. We just need to channel it.

It won't be easy, to be clear. Organizing is hard when you don't have, as conservatives do, a hate object to organize around. But liberals do have the advantage in that our values—social justice, economic fairness, gender equality—have, by and large, won the public argument. It's one reason that the right has been reduced to one-note trolling, because they know they can't win an actual debate about values. That's a strength. And if we treat it like one and put in the hard work, we can get our already existing coalition into an organized form that can fight back.

And don't underestimate how a little bit of anger, particularly at Trump and his deplorable supporters, can help give the left the little boost it so badly needs. So long as we hang on to our values, there's little danger of liberals turning into a troll nation of their own.

ALSO AVAILABLE FROM
HOT BOOKS

AN IMPRINT OF SKYHORSE PUBLISHING

The Gilded Rage
A Wild Ride Through Donald Trump's America
Alexander Zaitchik
Foreword by David Talbot
$21.99| Hardcover | ISBN: 978-1-5107-1428-1

2016 was one of the most surreal and unpredictable election years in modern history and this is due in large part to one Donald J. Trump and the millions of Americans who made him president. President Trump succeeded despite behavior that would cripple any other politician. It is imperative to understand why so many continue to support him. And this is what makes *The Gilded Rage* so important; it provides insight into the forgotten Americans that continue to befuddle pundits and "experts" on CNN and FOX alike.

This grippingly intimate and heart-breaking book provides a portrait of the walking wounded who make up the base of the Trump movement, who have watched their fortunes dwindle with each passing year. These men and women feel forgotten and screwed over by political, corporate, and media elites . . . and they feel that Donald Trump, despite his flamboyant demagoguery, might well be their last chance for salvation. Alexander Zaitchik in this important book takes us deeper into the ravaged soul of America than any other chronicler of our times.

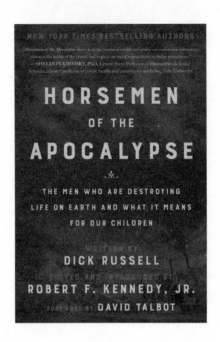

Horsemen of the Apocalypse
The Men Who Are Destroying Life on Earth—And What It Means for Our Children
Dick Russell
Edited and Introduced by Robert F. Kennedy Jr.
Foreword by David Talbot
$21.99| Hardcover | ISBN: 978-1-5107-0334-6

The science is overwhelming; the facts are in. The planet is heating up at an alarming rate, and the results are everywhere to be seen. Yet, as time runs out, climate progress is blocked by the men who are profiting from the burning of the planet: energy moguls like the Koch brothers and former Exxon Mobil CEO Rex Tillerson. Powerful politicians like senators Mitch McConnell and Jim Inhofe, who receive massive contributions from the oil and coal industries.

Most of these men are too intelligent to truly believe that climate change is not a growing crisis. And yet they have put their profits and careers ahead of the health and welfare of the world's population—and even their own children and grandchildren. *Horsemen of the Apocalypse* takes a personal look at this global crisis, literally bringing it home.

Unspeakable
Talks with David Talbot About the Most Forbidden Topics
in America

Chris Hedges with David Talbot
$21.99| Hardcover | ISBN: 978-1-5107-1273-7

The mainstream media reacted with shock at the rise of Donald Trump on the right and Bernie Sanders on the left during the 2016 presidential race. But Chris Hedges has been shining a light on the most overlooked people and issues for nearly four decades. Now, he addresses these burning topics in a rare, extended conversation with fellow radical journalist David Talbot.

Hedges talks about his personal odyssey, from middle-class scholarship student at elite prep schools and Ivy League colleges to his years as a war correspondent; from his turbulent career at the *New York Times* to his rebirth as a truth-telling, bestselling author in the tradition of George Orwell, James Baldwin, and Noam Chomsky.

Along the way, Hedges offers his unvarnished views on topics rarely aired by the corporate media, including the hopeless corruption of our political system, the difficulty of challenging the prevailing story lines of elite consensus, the disturbing parallels between current US conditions and the collapse of Balkans society into fascist violence during the 1990s, and the criminalization of poverty. All of which is to say, Chris Hedges is unafraid to say what is necessary and true—and has always been. We must listen to him and the urgent message he brings in this book.